ANXIETY AND PHOBIAS

GENERAL EDITORS

Dale C. Garell, M.D.
Medical Director, California Children Services, Department of Health Services,
    County of Los Angeles
Associate Dean for Curriculum; Clinical Professor, Department of Pediatrics &
    Family Medicine, University of Southern California School of Medicine
Former President, Society for Adolescent Medicine

Solomon H. Snyder, M.D.
Distinguished Service Professor of Neuroscience, Pharmacology, and Psychiatry,
    Johns Hopkins University School of Medicine
Former President, Society for Neuroscience
Albert Lasker Award in Medical Research, 1978

CONSULTING EDITORS

Robert W. Blum, M.D., Ph.D.
Professor and Director, Division of General Pediatrics and Adolescent Health,
    University of Minnesota

Charles E. Irwin, Jr., M.D.
Professor of Pediatrics; Director, Division of Adolescent Medicine, University of
    California, San Francisco

Lloyd J. Kolbe, Ph.D.
Director of the Division of Adolescent and School Health, Center for Chronic
    Disease Prevention and Health Promotion, Centers for Disease Control

Jordan J. Popkin
Director, Division of Federal Employee Occupational Health, U.S. Public Health
    Service Region I

Joseph L. Rauh, M.D.
Professor of Pediatrics and Medicine, Adolescent Medicine, Children's Hospital
    Medical Center, Cincinnati
Former President, Society for Adolescent Medicine

THE ENCYCLOPEDIA OF
HEALTH

PSYCHOLOGICAL DISORDERS AND THEIR TREATMENT

Solomon H. Snyder, M.D. · General Editor

ANXIETY AND PHOBIAS

Don Nardo

Introduction by C. Everett Koop, M.D., Sc.D.

former Surgeon General, U.S. Public Health Service

CHELSEA HOUSE PUBLISHERS

New York · Philadelphia

The goal of the ENCYCLOPEDIA OF HEALTH *is to provide general information in the ever-changing areas of physiology, psychology, and related medical issues. The titles in this series are not intended to take the place of the professional advice of a physician or other health care professional.*

ON THE COVER: *Age of Anxiety,* © 1991, R. Patrick Sullivan

CHELSEA HOUSE PUBLISHERS
EDITOR-IN-CHIEF   Remmel Nunn
MANAGING EDITOR   Karyn Gullen Browne
COPY CHIEF   Mark Rifkin
PICTURE EDITOR   Adrian G. Allen
ART DIRECTOR   Maria Epes
ASSISTANT ART DIRECTOR   Noreen Romano
MANUFACTURING DIRECTOR   Gerald Levine
SYSTEMS MANAGER   Lindsey Ottman
PRODUCTION MANAGER   Joseph Romano
PRODUCTION COORDINATOR   Marie Claire Cebrián

The Encyclopedia of Health
SENIOR EDITOR   Brian Feinberg

Staff for ANXIETY AND PHOBIAS
ASSOCIATE EDITOR   LaVonne Carlson-Finnerty
SENIOR COPY EDITOR   Laurie Kahn
EDITORIAL ASSISTANT   Tamar Levovitz
PICTURE RESEARCHER   Pat Burns
DESIGNER   Robert Yaffe

First Printing
1   3   5   7   9   8   6   4   2

Library of Congress Cataloging-in-Publication Data

Nardo, Don.
    Anxiety and phobias/by Don Nardo; introduction by C. Everett Koop.
        p. cm.—(The Encyclopedia of health. Psychological disorders and their treatment)
    Includes bibliographical references and index.
    Summary: Examines the various types and causes of anxiety and phobias and the methods used to treat them.
    ISBN 0-7910-0041-9
            0-7910-0508-9 (pbk.)
1. Phobias—Juvenile literature. 2. Anxiety—Juvenile literature. [1. Phobias.
2. Anxiety. 3. Fear.] I. Title. II. Series.   91-22876
RC535.N37 1991   CIP
616.85'22—dc20   AC

CONTENTS

PREVENTION AND EDUCATION: THE KEYS TO GOOD HEALTH

C. Everett Koop, M.D., Sc.D.
former Surgeon General,
U.S. Public Health Service

The issue of health education has received particular attention in recent years because of the presence of AIDS in the news. But our response to this particular tragedy points up a number of broader issues that doctors, public health officials, educators, and the public face. In particular, it points up the necessity for sound health education for citizens of all ages.

Over the past 25 years this country has been able to bring about dramatic declines in the death rates for heart disease, stroke, accidents, and for people under the age of 45, cancer. Today, Americans generally eat better and take better care of themselves than ever before. Thus, with the help of modern science and technology, they have a better chance of surviving serious—even catastrophic—illnesses. That's the good news.

But, like every phonograph record, there's a flip side, and one with special significance for young adults. According to a report issued in 1979 by Dr. Julius Richmond, my predecessor as Surgeon General, Americans aged 15 to 24 had a higher death rate in 1979 than they did 20 years earlier. The causes: violent death and injury, alcohol and drug abuse, unwanted pregnancies, and sexually transmitted diseases. Adolescents are particularly vulnerable because they are beginning to explore their own sexuality and perhaps to experiment with drugs. The need for educating young people is critical, and the price of neglect is high.

Yet even for the population as a whole, our health is still far from what it could be. Why? A 1974 Canadian government report attributed all death and disease to four broad elements: inadequacies in the health care system, behavioral factors or unhealthy life-styles, environmental hazards, and human biological factors.

To be sure, there are diseases that are still beyond the control of even our advanced medical knowledge and techniques. And despite yearnings that are as old as the human race itself, there is no "fountain of youth" to ward off aging and death. Still, there is a solution to many of the problems that undermine sound health. In a word, that solution is prevention. Prevention, which includes health promotion and education, saves lives, improves the quality of life, and in the long run, saves money.

In the United States, organized public health activities and preventive medicine have a long history. Important milestones in this country or foreign breakthroughs adopted in the United States include the improvement of sanitary procedures and the development of pasteurized milk in the late 19th century and the introduction in the mid-20th century of effective vaccines against polio, measles, German measles, mumps, and other once-rampant diseases. Internationally, organized public health efforts began on a wide-scale basis with the International Sanitary Conference of 1851, to which 12 nations sent representatives. The World Health Organization, founded in 1948, continues these efforts under the aegis of the United Nations, with particular emphasis on combating communicable diseases and the training of health care workers.

Despite these accomplishments, much remains to be done in the field of prevention. For too long, we have had a medical care system that is science- and technology-based, focused, essentially, on illness and mortality. It is now patently obvious that both the social and the economic costs of such a system are becoming insupportable.

Implementing prevention—and its corollaries, health education and promotion—is the job of several groups of people.

First, the medical and scientific professions need to continue basic scientific research, and here we are making considerable progress. But increased concern with prevention will also have a decided impact on how primary care doctors practice medicine. With a shift to health-based rather than morbidity-based medicine, the role of the "new physician" will include a healthy dose of patient education.

Second, practitioners of the social and behavioral sciences—psychologists, economists, city planners—along with lawyers, business leaders, and government officials—must solve the practical and ethical dilemmas confronting us: poverty, crime, civil rights, literacy, education, employment, housing, sanitation, environmental protection, health care delivery systems, and so forth. All of these issues affect public health.

Third is the public at large. We'll consider that very important group in a moment.

Fourth, and the linchpin in this effort, is the public health profession—doctors, epidemiologists, teachers—who must harness the professional expertise of the first two groups and the common sense and cooperation of the third, the public. They must define the problems statistically and qualitatively and then help us set priorities for finding the solutions.

To a very large extent, improving those statistics is the responsibility of every individual. So let's consider more specifically what the role of the individual should be and why health education is so important to that role. First, and most obvious, individuals can protect themselves from illness and injury and thus minimize their need for professional medical care. They can eat nutritious food; get adequate exercise; avoid tobacco, alcohol, and drugs; and take prudent steps to avoid accidents. The proverbial "apple a day keeps the doctor away" is not so far from the truth, after all.

Second, individuals should actively participate in their own medical care. They should schedule regular medical and dental checkups. Should they develop an illness or injury, they should know when to treat themselves and when to seek professional help. To gain the maximum benefit from any medical treatment that they do require, individuals must become partners in that treatment. For instance, they should understand the effects and side effects of medications. I counsel young physicians that there is no such thing as too much information when talking with patients. But the corollary is the patient must know enough about the nuts and bolts of the healing process to understand what the doctor is telling him or her. That is at least partially the patient's responsibility.

Education is equally necessary for us to understand the ethical and public policy issues in health care today. Sometimes individuals will encounter these issues in making decisions about their own treatment or that of family members. Other citizens may encounter them as jurors in medical malpractice cases. But we all become involved, indirectly, when we elect our public officials, from school board members to the president. Should surrogate parenting be legal? To what extent is drug testing desirable, legal, or necessary? Should there be public funding for family planning, hospitals, various types of medical research, and other medical care for the indigent? How should we allocate scant technological resources, such as kidney dialysis and organ transplants? What is the proper role of government in protecting the rights of patients?

What are the broad goals of public health in the United States today? In 1980, the Public Health Service issued a report aptly entitled *Promoting Health—Preventing Disease: Objectives for the Nation*. This report expressed its goals in terms of mortality and in terms of intermediate goals in education and health improvement. It identified 15 major concerns: controlling high blood pressure; improving family planning; improving pregnancy care and infant health; increasing the rate of immunization; controlling sexually transmitted diseases; controlling the presence of toxic agents and radiation in the environment; improving occupational safety and health; preventing accidents; promoting water fluoridation and dental health; controlling infectious diseases; decreasing smoking; decreasing alcohol and drug abuse; improving nutrition; promoting physical fitness and exercise; and controlling stress and violent behavior.

For healthy adolescents and young adults (ages 15 to 24), the specific goal was a 20% reduction in deaths, with a special focus on motor vehicle injuries and alcohol and drug abuse. For adults (ages 25 to 64), the aim was 25% fewer deaths, with a concentration on heart attacks, strokes, and cancers.

Smoking is perhaps the best example of how individual behavior can have a direct impact on health. Today, cigarette smoking is recognized as the single most important preventable cause of death in our society. It is responsible for more cancers and more cancer deaths than any other known agent; is a prime risk factor for heart and blood vessel disease, chronic bronchitis, and emphysema; and is a frequent cause of complications in pregnancies and of babies born prematurely, underweight, or with potentially fatal respiratory and cardiovascular problems.

Since the release of the Surgeon General's first report on smoking in 1964, the proportion of adult smokers has declined substantially, from 43% in 1965 to 30.5% in 1985. Since 1965, 37 million people have quit smoking. Although there is still much work to be done if we are to become a "smoke-free society," it is heartening to note that public health and public education efforts—such as warnings on cigarette packages and bans on broadcast advertising—have already had significant effects.

In 1835, Alexis de Tocqueville, a French visitor to America, wrote, "In America the passion for physical well-being is general." Today, as then, health and fitness are front-page items. But with the greater scientific and technological resources now available to us, we are in a far stronger position to make good health care available to everyone. And with the greater technological threats to us as we approach the 21st century, the need to do so is more urgent than ever before. Comprehensive information about basic biology, preventive medicine, medical and surgical treatments, and related ethical and public policy issues can help you arm yourself with the knowledge you need to be healthy throughout your life.

FOREWORD

Solomon H. Snyder, M.D.

Mental disorders represent the number one health problem for the United States and probably for the entire human population. Some studies estimate that approximately one-third of all Americans suffer from some sort of emotional disturbance. Depression of varying severity will affect as many as 20% of all of us at one time or another in our lives. Severe anxiety is even more common.

Adolescence is a time of particular susceptibility to emotional problems. Teenagers are undergoing significant changes in their brain as well as their physical structure. The hormones that alter the organs of reproduction during puberty also influence the way we think and feel. At a purely psychological level, adolescents must cope with major upheavals in their lives. After years of not noticing the opposite sex, they find themselves romantically attracted but must painfully learn the skills of social interchange both for superficial, flirtatious relationships and for genuine intimacy. Teenagers must develop new ways of relating to their parents. Adolescents strive for independence. Yet, our society is structured in such a way that teenagers must remain dependent on their parents for many more years. During adolescence, young men and women examine their own intellectual bents and begin to plan the type of higher education and vocation they believe they will find most fulfilling.

Because of these challenges, teenagers are more emotionally volatile than adults. Passages from extreme exuberance to dejection are common. The emotional distress of completely normal adolescence can be so severe that the same disability in an adult would be labeled as major mental illness. Although most teenagers somehow muddle through and emerge unscathed, a number of problems are more frequent among adolescents than among adults. Many psychological aberrations reflect severe disturbances, although these are sometimes not regarded as "psychiatric." Eating disorders, to which young adults are especially vulnerable, are an example. An extremely large number of teenagers diet to great excess even though they are not overweight. Many of them suffer from a specific disturbance referred to as anorexia nervosa, a form of self-starvation that is just as real a disorder as diabetes. The same is true for those who eat compulsively and then sometimes force themselves to vomit. They may be afflicted with bulimia.

Depression is also surprisingly frequent among adolescents, although its symptoms may be less obvious in young people than they are in adults. And, because suicide occurs most frequently in those suffering from depression, we must be on the lookout for subtle hints of despondency in those close to us. This is especially urgent because teenage suicide is a rapidly worsening national problem.

The volumes on Psychological Disorders and Their Treatment in the ENCYCLOPEDIA OF HEALTH cover the major areas of mental illness, from mild to severe. They also emphasize the means available for getting help. *Anxiety and Phobias, Depression,* and *Schizophrenia* deal specifically with these forms of mental disturbance. *Child Abuse* and *Delinquency and Criminal Behavior* explore abnormalities of behavior that may stem from environmental and social influences as much as from biological or psychological illness. *Personality Disorders* and *Compulsive Behavior* explain how people develop disturbances of their overall personality. *Learning Disabilities* investigates disturbances of the mind that may reflect neurological derangements as much as psychological abnormalities. *Mental Retardation* explains the various causes of this many-sided handicap, including the genetic component, complications during pregnancy, and traumas during birth. *Suicide* discusses the epidemiology of this tragic phenomenon and outlines the assistance available to those who are at risk. *Stress Management* locates the source of stress in contemporary society and considers formal strategies for coping with it. Finally, *Diagnosing and Treating Mental Illness* explains to the reader how professionals sift through various signs and symptoms to define the exact nature of the various mental disorders and fully describes the most effective means of alleviating them.

Fortunately, when it comes to psychological disorders, knowing the facts is a giant step toward solving the problems.

CHAPTER 1

THE AGE OF ANXIETY

The Age of Anxiety *is the title of this 1953 painting by Ben Shahn. The* terms age of anxiety *and* century of fear *are often used to describe the 20th century.*

The 20th century has often been called the Age of Anxiety. This was the title of composer-conductor Leonard Bernstein's Second Symphony. It was also the title of a 1947 volume by the well-known poet W. H. Auden. In the same year, the French writer Albert Camus described modern times as "the century of fear."

Yet *anxiety*, an uneasy feeling of apprehension, is not peculiar to this century or to any other. References to the problem can be detected in ancient Egyptian hieroglyphics, and medieval writers referred to anxiety as "a basic condition of human existence."

✱ WHAT IS ANXIETY?

Specialists who study the workings of the human mind generally describe anxiety as fear due to stress. The stress may be emotional in nature, as when a person is distressed about a death in the family. The stress might be related to physical problems, such as an injury or serious disease, or it may be chemically induced, as when someone is affected by hormonal changes. Any kind of stress can create a state of anxiety.

In its simplest and mildest form, anxiety is a physical and emotional expression of a person's fear. Anxiety and fear are very similar emotions, but the source of these feelings is what sets them apart. Whereas normal fears are responses to actual events, anxiety usually involves the anticipation of a negative situation. The cause of anxiety is often vague and unspecified. If the feeling of apprehension remains after its cause is known, it is then referred to as worry.

One example of the difference between normal fear and anxiety is *test anxiety*, a condition faced by many students when taking an exam. Test anxiety usually affects students whose grades are in the medium range but who become so full of self-doubt that they can hardly concentrate on the test. Usually the student has studied for the test but is not certain that he or she is properly prepared and is therefore nagged by feelings of anxiety. If, after the test is turned in and all the answers

These stockbrokers are used to the stress on the trading floor. Stress and the anxiety that accompanies it are a typical part of most people's everyday life.

This 1792 illustration by Thomas Rowlandson depicts The Hypochondriac, *a patient who imagines she is ill, although no real physical problem exists. This type of disorder is referred to as disguised anxiety.*

have been completed, he or she expects the worst result, the condition is considered worry. On the other hand, a student who forgets to study and is totally unprepared approaches the test with a natural amount of fear—he or she did not study, so it is likely that the test will be difficult.

Typical physical symptoms of anxiety include muscle tension, increased heart rate, shortness of breath, dry mouth, and a cold, clammy feeling on the skin. When anxiety is manifested mentally, the person's attention narrows, and he or she tends to focus on the discomfort, feeling irritable and unsure of what will happen next.

This sort of anxiety may be considered a normal reaction under stressful circumstances. Everyone feels anxiety at one time or another, and sometimes it is actually beneficial. It can help a person realize that danger is present and prepare him or her to escape it. Because it forces an individual to concentrate on the emergency at hand, anxiety may help someone solve an urgent problem. However, when a person's fear seems far greater and lasts much longer than a problem warrants, he or she is experiencing an *anxiety disorder.*

ANXIETY DISORDERS

Anxiety disorders are expressed in different ways, depending on the individual's personality and his or her degree of fear. A number of terms are used to describe specific conditions of the problem, but they all fit into the larger category of *anxiety neuroses* (a term often used interchangeably with anxiety disorders). A neurosis is a condition in which a person experiences emotional distress with no apparent cause. The disturbance affects part of the individual's personality without causing a total distortion.

Anxiety neuroses are further divided into categories that correspond to the severity of anxiety symptoms, including *generalized*

The face in Paul Klee's 1933 painting, Un Savant, *suggests the uneasy feeling that accompanies a generalized anxiety disorder, a condition wherein a person constantly worries about a minor or nonexistent problem.*

The Scream *by Edvard Munch dramatically depicts a severe state of fear. A person who experiences panic attacks can easily relate to the feeling illustrated by the artist.*

anxiety disorder, *panic attacks*, and *phobias*. Severe anxiety may also take another form called *disguised anxiety*, which often appears in the form of *hypochondria*, a condition wherein an individual falsely believes that he or she is ill.

Generalized Anxiety Disorder

Generalized anxiety disorder occurs when an individual suffers excessive anxiety and worry about possible misfortunes. Although the cause of concern may seem realistic, such as fear of financial or physical difficulties, it is the degree of ongoing anxiety that makes this a serious disorder. These concerns are often directed at a threat that is minimal or even nonexistent.

Symptoms of generalized anxiety disorder are more intense than those associated with everyday anxiety. The individual may experience an increased heart rate, shortness of breath, dry mouth, and abdominal tension or pain and may also feel weak and dizzy, become pale, and begin to tremble and sweat. In addition, the individual often grows irritable and overly tense, developing insomnia and having difficulty concentrating. Yet this sort of anxiety is not considered severe because the person may continue to function normally in everyday affairs.

Panic Attacks

When extreme symptoms of anxiety occur suddenly and the individual also feels a loss of control that causes him or her to act irrationally, the experience is called a panic attack. (The term *anxiety attack* is also used to describe this condition.) The sufferer often believes that serious injury or death is imminent and seeks to escape from the disturbing circumstances at any cost. These attacks usually last several minutes but may sometimes continue for hours. They may or may not accompany phobias.

Phobias

A phobia is an overpowering fear that involves an extreme and irrational dread of a certain object, activity, or situation. When faced with the object that he or she dreads, a phobic person cannot be convinced that everything is all right. Although he or she is often aware that the fear is irrational, the person cannot talk him- or herself out of being afraid. The condition has automatic reactions that come from within and require tremendous effort to overcome.

Many people are ashamed of their phobias, yet they need not be. Phobias are not a sign of mental or physical weakness, and anyone—no matter how strong and rugged—can be affected by them. In fact, many

U.S. Adults – By Selected Mental Disorder

Mental disorder	1-month		6-month		Lifetime	
	Number*	Percent	Number*	Percent	Number*	Percent
Anxiety disorders	13.1	7.3%	16.2	9.0%	26.0	14.6%
Phobia	11.2	6.2%	14.0	8.0%	22.5	12.5%
Obsessive-compulsive disorder	2.3	1.3%	2.7	1.5%	4.5	2.5%
Panic disorder	0.9	0.5%	1.8	1.0%	2.9	1.6%

*In millions

Source: National Institute of Mental Health

Anxiety and phobias are among today's most prevalent mental disorders. This chart illustrates the percentage of anxiety disorders that affected the adult population over different lengths of time in 1987.

"average" individuals of every race, religion, and educational background suffer from one or more phobias at some time in their life. Fear of heights, enclosed spaces, or public places affect millions of people each year in the United States alone. A study by the Office of Scientific Information at the National Institute of Mental Health revealed that 7.3% of the American population reported anxiety disorders that lasted for at least one month during 1987.

Anxiety and Phobias—The Difference

Anxiety and phobias are related, but they are not interchangeable. Because phobias are specific fears that display symptoms of anxiety, some level of anxiety is always present in phobic reactions. Phobias are thought to result from deep feelings of anxiety that are directed toward the dreaded object or situation. Yet many cases of severe anxiety do not produce phobias.

Phobias occur relatively rarely as compared to anxiety, a feeling that many people encounter quite often. Although anxiety is a common feeling, many people do not recognize its presence. It can be difficult to identify because it typically has no obvious cause. Unlike grief or happiness, anxiety is a feeling that does not evoke visible signals, such as tears or laughter. Yet a person who becomes extremely anxious and does not seek relief may develop more severe anxiety problems, including phobias, which will be closely examined in the following chapters.

CHAPTER 2

WHAT IS A PHOBIA?

This Rowlandson cartoon illustrates a patient whose fears are taken to extremes. It suggests the irrational nature of phobic fears, which are often provoked by nonthreatening objects or imagined situations.

Sometimes people confuse phobias with anxiety or lump the two problems together as a single condition. However, such assumptions are incorrect. Phobias are unreasonable and persistent fears that focus on a specific object, animal, activity, or situation. They are accompanied by anxiety, a state of emotional and physical discomfort produced in reaction to stress.

Some phobias are common and well known, such as *acrophobia*, the fear of heights; *claustrophobia*, the fear of enclosed spaces; and *hematophobia*, the fear of blood. Other phobias are more obscure and unusual. For example, people who are frightened of shadows suffer from *sciophobia* and are referred to as *sciophobes*. Individuals who fear various forms of machinery suffer from *mechanophobia*, and those terrified of fish are *ichthyophobes*. Extreme fear of the devil is known as *Satanophobia*, and fear of ugliness is *dysmorephobia*. There is even a fear of going to bed—*clinophobia*.

Hundreds of little-known phobias have been documented by *psychologists* (specialists trained to treat mental disorders) and *psychiatrists* (medical doctors schooled in treating mental illness and authorized to prescribe drugs as part of therapy). Although many of these fears may seem bizarre and even a bit ridiculous to people who have never experienced phobic reactions, the problems are agonizingly

Some fears are valid, but others are imagined. Phobias often involve fearful anticipation—a person thinks ahead and then expects and even envisions the worst possible outcome for a situation.

real to those who suffer from them. Doctors recommend that all phobias be taken seriously and the victims treated sympathetically.

The gravity of the problem has been well illustrated with statistics. According to the American Psychiatric Association, at least 15 million people in the United States suffer from phobias of one kind or another. Of these people, as many as 1 million cannot function well enough to leave their own home. One of the saddest aspects of the problem is that most phobic people are aware that their fears are irrational. Unfortunately, this awareness makes them feel ashamed and afraid to seek help.

FEAR—NORMAL OR PHOBIC?

Phobic people rarely use the word *fear* to describe their feelings during a phobic reaction. They use more dramatic words, such as "horror" and "panic." Some insist that even these terms are not strong enough to convey the overwhelming sense of helplessness and terror that grips them. Typical descriptions include: "It was so bad I couldn't stand it"; "I thought I'd go out of my mind"; or "I thought I was going to die." According to psychologists, these reactions signify the difference between normal and phobic fears.

This ancient mosaic shows Death pointing to the motto Recognize Yourself. At the moment when anxiety sufferers are overcome by a panic attack, they often feel certain that they are about to die—an unlikely outcome.

Phobic fear is not just more intense than regular fear; it is a completely different type of experience. According to Manuel Zane in his book *Your Phobia*,

> Normal fear is a reaction to a definite perceived danger, real or conjectured. The cause of the fear is identified and the response is more or less controlled. In phobic fear the danger is not apparent, not recognized. All that is sensed is an overwhelming dread, without any apparent cause. The response is uncontrolled, mounting quickly to the level of unbounded panic.

Zane uses two case histories to illustrate his point. In the first, John J., a storekeeper, is getting ready to close up shop and go home. Suddenly, a stranger enters, threatens John with a gun, and demands that John give him the money in the cash register. John, realizing his life is in danger, experiences what experts refer to as a normal fear

A major difference between normal and phobic fears is what causes them. This young woman, who was taken hostage after a 1988 bank robbery in West Germany, experienced a normal fear reaction that probably disappeared after she was out of danger.

reaction. He tries to remain calm, but his heart pounds and his mouth goes dry. He becomes a bit light-headed, begins to perspire, and experiences shortness of breath. He also has a sick feeling in his stomach, and his hands tremble. Obviously, John is experiencing many classic physical symptoms of anxiety.

When the gunman leaves, John's fear begins to subside. Because he is no longer in danger, the physical and emotional responses triggered by the frightening encounter quickly disappear. John's breathing and heart rate return to normal, and he no longer perspires or trembles.

Now consider Zane's description of a woman whose fear is not normal. Anne T., a mother in her thirties, spends much of her time sitting on a wooden chair in her living room, crying. She is terrified that her house is overrun with bugs. Her husband insists that the place is not infested, but that does not console her. Anne refuses to sit on the upholstered furniture because she believes that dozens of hideous insects will dart from under the pillows and crawl over her body. When she or the children need something to eat, she runs into the kitchen, snatches food from the refrigerator or cabinet, then rushes out again. Anne is convinced that she will see a cockroach or silverfish crawl out from under the sink. When she does occasionally see a real insect, she panics and, according to her husband, does irrational things.

Anne T. often experiences the very same anxiety symptoms John J. felt when his store was being robbed. But two significant differences separate his normal fear reaction from her phobic reaction. First, John's response to fear was, more or less, controlled. Although he experienced physical responses (pounding heart, dry mouth), he recognized what the danger was and knew what to do in order to keep himself from being injured or killed. In contrast, Anne's fears are uncontrolled. She does not know if or when the danger will actually appear or how to protect herself against it.

∗ The second difference between the two types of fear is the real, or tangible, nature of the danger. In John's case, the danger was obviously real. The man with the gun stood before him, threatening him verbally and physically. Anne, on the other hand, reacts constantly to a nonexistent threat. She has been shown time and again that her house is not

When a phobia becomes extreme, an individual limits his or her activities in order to avoid the object or situation that triggers feelings of
dread. The person may grow so desperate to stay away from anything associated with the fear that he or she becomes isolated, a
situation expressed by Munch in Melancholy.

infested, yet she continues to exhibit feelings of overwhelming dread.
She repeatedly attempts to escape the "danger" by avoiding it.

Avoidance Behavior

Normal *avoidance behavior* occurs when a person seeks to minimize
possible trouble by staying away from potential danger. This behavior
is natural. For instance, if people know that there have been muggings
on a dark street in a violent neighborhood, they will avoid walking on
that street. Similarly, reported sightings of sharks near a public beach
will convince a majority of people to stay out of the water even if they
themselves have not seen the sharks. For most people, avoidance
behavior is simply a matter of taking sensible precautions.

Phobic people also practice avoidance. Similar to the case of Anne
T., a *claustrophobe* does everything possible to stay away from closets,
elevators, and other enclosed spaces. A person with *aviophobia*, the

fear of flying, practices avoidance by refusing to set foot on an airplane. According to doctors, avoidance is not a problem if the behavior succeeds in eliminating phobic reactions and does not significantly disrupt the person's life.

However, with phobic people there is always the danger that avoidance behavior will increase. The person may become so obsessed with staying out of harm's way that fear begins to control his or her life. First, the subject avoids only those objects or situations that are directly related to a specific phobia. But, little by little, the person perceives that other seemingly harmless situations might somehow lead to "dangerous" ones, so he or she begins to form a very elaborate pattern designed to stay as far from danger as possible. Finally, as one phobic person explained, "You are a prisoner inside your own walls, cut off from everything and everyone on the outside."

Harry M., who suffered from a fear of flying, experienced the development of this sort of elaborate and destructive avoidance pattern. After suffering a terrible panic attack on an airplane, he began to view the airport as an object of terror. Weeks later, he began to avoid the bridge leading to the airport because he associated it with his bad experience on the plane. "Eventually," Harry said, "I was afraid to cross over any bridges at all. They all reminded me of the one going to the airport."

Soon Harry began to avoid certain buildings because they seemed somehow related to the bridges, and then he completely refused to drive. "In the end," Harry admitted, "I just wanted to be in my house. Sometimes, only my bedroom felt completely safe. I gave up all my usual activities. . . . I felt so helpless, I eventually moved back to my parents' house."

Types of Phobias

There is no simple, universally accepted way to classify the numerous phobias reported by doctors. Different experts categorize phobias in various ways. For instance, many doctors group together phobias involving single objects and refer to them as *simple phobias*. Some include animal phobias in this group. It is also common practice to lump together phobias involving people or public situations and call them *social phobias*, although not all experts use this term.

The following chapter will examine *agoraphobia*, a condition with no apparent cause (it is not triggered by a specific object or situation) which results in such extreme fear that it is often referred to as "the fear of fear." Experts agree that agoraphobia is the most severe and debilitating phobia. For that reason, they usually put it in its own category. Because it is so consuming, many studies of phobias concentrate solely on this overwhelming and terrifying condition.

CHAPTER 3

THE FEAR
OF FEAR

Agoraphobia is not specifically a fear of open spaces but an over- whelming sense of terror and a fear that the situation is inescapable.

For many people who suffer from anxiety and phobias, a panic attack is the experience they dread most, even more than the object or situation that creates the fear. The attacks may happen at any time, in any locaton, often with little warning—which only increases the phobic's fear of them. These panic attacks are a primary symptom in many cases of agoraphobia. The following account illustrates how a panic attack can severely restrict a person's everyday life. According to Connie V., an electronics assembler in her late thirties:

The panic attacks I experience usually take place in public locations, such as a shopping mall, grocery store, bank, or driving on the freeway. I will often feel anxiety just thinking about doing any of these things. For instance, when I decide to go to the mall, I start to get feelings of anxiety and apprehension. The closer I get to the mall, the stronger these feelings become. Once inside the mall, I may or may not get a panic attack, and it may vary from mild to severe. The symptoms include shaking, sweating, heart pounding, loss of balance, difficulty in thinking clearly, an overall feeling of dread, and a very strong desire to get out of the mall as quickly as possible. Even though I know that this response makes no sense, it can be impossible to control. It is not the mall I am afraid of. It is the fear that being in the mall will bring on a panic attack. There is no way for me to put into words the deep fear an attack can cause, even though I know it is irrational.

THE MODERN VIEW OF AGORAPHOBIA

Experts often consider agoraphobia the most severe form of anxiety disorder. The first researcher to describe the condition was the German neurologist Dr. Karl Westphal in 1871, after he encountered three unrelated cases of people who complained that they felt terrified for no apparent reason. The terror struck them in the middle of the day as they went about their usual routine, working and shopping, and each of them felt safe only after returning home.

Westphal defined the condition as the "impossibility of walking through certain streets or places [without feeling] dread or anxiety." In naming the condition, he combined two Greek words—*agora*, meaning marketplace, and *phobia*, meaning dread.

For several years after Westphal studied agoraphobia, other doctors who described the problem tended to oversimplify it. They usually referred to it as a "fear of open places"—a definition that caught on. However, most experts now agree that this is not an accurate description. First, they say, agoraphobia is not a simple fear but an all-consuming dread. Second, people do not have to be in open, unprotected places to experience the condition.

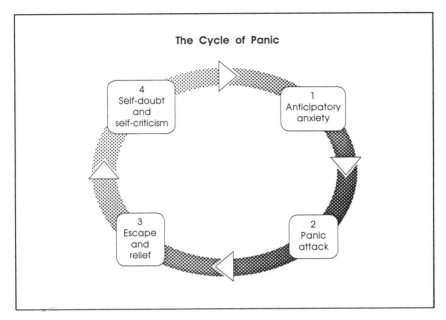

The Cycle of Panic

4
Self-doubt
and
self-criticism

1
Anticipatory
anxiety

3
Escape
and
relief

2
Panic
attack

Panic attacks may create a vicious cycle of fear. A person's fear of a possible attack may become so intense that it actually causes the attack to occur. The person then becomes even more afraid of another recurrence, and the fear intensifies.

Agoraphobes may suffer panic attacks in closed spaces, low places, underwater, or, in fact, anywhere. Whether the person is in a shopping center, on a bridge, in an elevator, in a church, in an airplane, or in some other location, the result is always the same: When panic strikes, the agoraphobe feels that he or she must escape that location and find the safety of home.

One of the most frightening aspects of the attacks is their unpredictability—the victim never knows when or where the next attack might occur. If the attacks persist, the sufferer may develop an intense dread of the attacks themselves, a condition called *anticipatory anxiety*. This occurs when a person suffers heightened anxiety caused by the fear of a possible recurrence of the attacks. This fear creates a seemingly inescapable cycle of dread followed by attacks, followed by more dread and more attacks. Fortunately, this cycle occurs only in those who suffer from agoraphobia.

Another result of agoraphobia is that it leads to the repeated avoidance of any situation in which a person may experience this extreme fear. In many cases, agoraphobia involves several different phobias. An agoraphobic person can and usually does suffer from two or more phobias that combine to create the overwhelming condition of dread called agoraphobia. Eventually, an agoraphobe may choose to stay home rather than risk facing his or her fears in a public situation.

When a person suffers from just one phobia, he or she can escape the one thing that causes the fear and then continue normally in other areas of life. But an agoraphobe feels threatened from many directions at once. One terrible experience leads to another until the agoraphobe believes that the only remedy is to retreat into a tiny, isolated sanctum— usually his or her home.

DIFFERENCES IN EVERY CASE

Agoraphobia appears in many variations and affects each victim differently. Some patients say that it took several years for the problem to become severe enough to restrict their life. Others claim that their dread escalated much more quickly, perhaps within a few months. Some people suffer from the condition constantly, whereas others seem to improve for a time and then relapse, finding that the problem has become even worse. This unpredictable fluctuation between normal and phobic phases may continue for years.

Most agoraphobes react to their problem by slowly restructuring their life as well as changing the routines of those surrounding them. Consider the case of Veronica F., as reported by Michael Goldstein and James Palmer in their book *The Experience of Anxiety*:

> For several months . . . Mrs. F. had been unable to leave her home without generalized feelings of panic, which she could not explain. [She said,] "It is as if something dreadful would happen to me if I did not immediately go home." Even after she would return to the house, she would feel shaken inside and unable to speak to anyone or do anything for an hour or so. However, as long as she remained in her own house or garden, she was able to carry out her routine life without much problem. . . . Mrs. F. stated that she had always been a

somewhat shy person who generally preferred keeping to herself, but that up until approximately a year ago she had always been able to go to her job, shop, or go to church without any particular feelings of dread or uneasiness.

Mrs. F. experienced her first panic attack in a public place while she was Christmas shopping:

> Standing in the middle of a crowded department store . . . she suddenly felt the impulse to flee. She . . . drove home as fast as she could. . . . Over the next several weeks . . . she had several similar attacks: at a church party, at a friend's house, on the way to the dentist, and even just going to the grocery store.

Eventually Mrs. F. gave up all her outside activities and retreated to her home, forcing her family to visit her there and nowhere else. Relatives also had to run her errands and constantly check to see that she was all right. In time, Mrs. F. began to feel better.

> She had stayed at home . . . during the entire summer . . . and her symptoms seldom appeared. However, as soon as it was necessary for her to return to work, her phobia returned even more intensely; she realized that she must get help.

Goldstein cites yet another example, involving a young pregnant woman from New York who had her first attack while on a train. When the woman first felt a painful tension in her abdomen, she thought she was having a miscarriage. She envisioned in vivid detail losing the baby and soon felt herself beginning to faint. She felt a tremendous urge to escape and got off the train at the nearest station, then called her husband to pick her up. It became obvious that the condition was panic when the woman's fear quickly spread to other forms of transportation, such as buses and cars. Fear of streets, stores, and other public areas followed. Finally, she retreated to her home, where she remained for five years.

DISTINGUISHING TRAITS

Although each specific case of agoraphobia is different, there are certain factors common to all those who suffer from the condition. For example, many agoraphobes are goal oriented and work hard to fulfill extremely high standards. They worry that they will fail somehow, which makes them work even harder. Many agoraphobes are perfectionists. This does not mean that all perfectionists are agoraphobic or in danger of becoming so. Yet it does suggest that people who constantly set unrealistic, unattainable goals for themselves may have more of a tendency toward agoraphobia than those who do not.

In *Your Phobia*, Zane notes that many people with agoraphobia tend to be overly sensitive about what others think of them. They express concerns such as "being embarrassed," "making a fool of myself," or "if people really knew the things I am thinking and feeling and doing, they'd think that I'm crazy." Agoraphobes often report that when they are experiencing an attack and feel unable to escape the notice of others, the attack worsens considerably. The fear that an attack might occur in the presence of others adds to the agoraphobe's desire to avoid public places.

Additionally, many agoraphobes were unusually fearful as children. They report having vivid, active imaginations as well as having parents who were overly nervous and fearful themselves. In *Your Phobia*, Mrs. M. describes her childhood to Zane:

Although the cause of agoraphobia is not known, many victims report having had extremely fearful childhoods that often included emotionally painful experiences. Munch depicts in The Dead Mother and the Child *a situation that many children find terrifying to consider.*

I was always a scared child. I had bad dreams, night after night. Many of them had to do with death. I was terribly afraid of dying. My mother was very neurotic. When I was sick, she would run out into the streets screaming that I was dying. When any one of us was sick, she used to run out of the house saying she couldn't take care of us, that we were too sick. That's where I got the idea I was going to die. As a child and teenager, I was a very nervous person. If I had a bloody nose or cut myself, I knew I was going to bleed to death. If I had the flu, I'd think I was dying.

At the age of 14, Mrs. M. had her first agoraphobic experience:

I was on a bus, all the way in the back and it was packed. All of a sudden, I panicked. I had to get to the front, where I could breathe. . . . I felt like I was lost. . . . After the bus incident, I didn't want to be in any crowded place because I couldn't breathe. . . . I used to miss a lot of time from school so I wouldn't have to go through the halls with all the kids. . . . I went to all sorts of doctors and got all sorts of hospital tests, and they all told me there was nothing wrong with me. But that didn't make me any less afraid.

Agoraphobia and Age

Although Mrs. M. experienced her first attack at age 14, most agoraphobes are afflicted when they are somewhat older. The condition usually begins in the mid- to late twenties, rarely appearing before age 18 or after age 35. This age difference distinguishes agoraphobia from simple and social phobias.

Simple phobias generally appear in childhood. For example, fears of animals usually appear in early childhood, before the age of seven, and often disappear before puberty. Social phobias typically begin during adolescence and rarely occur after age 30. A phobia that appears after the age of 30 may seem at first to be a simple or social phobia, yet these cases often prove to be agoraphobia or a symptom of depression.

The 1925 lithograph Heimarbeit (Homework), by Käthe Kollwitz, conveys the depression that surrounds those who feel trapped at home. Although depression often accompanies agoraphobia, doctors cannot identify a link between them.

AGORAPHOBIA AND DEPRESSION

Many agoraphobic people also suffer from *depression*, a condition wherein a person's mental and physical energy is low, or *depressed*. A depressed person feels sad, dejected, helpless, or a combination of these things. Often the person feels that there is no hope, that life is awful, and that there is no way to make it better.

Everyone feels mildly depressed at times, especially when something sad occurs, such as the death of a relative or friend. Yet after a few days or weeks, the average person copes with the problem, then bounces back and feels better. For an agoraphobe, however, depression lasts longer and is more severe.

A person may experience agoraphobia first, then become increasingly depressed when there seems to be no way to prevent the onset of fear and panic. Depression may also result when a loved one reacts badly to the phobic condition. This occurred in the case of Ethel H. In *Personality Development and Psychopathology*, Norman Cameron and Joseph Rychlak described how Ethel

> suffered her first acute anxiety attack [after] arriving alone by plane from England after visiting her parents there. As she entered the high-ceilinged terminal, where no one met her, she suddenly felt terrified at the huge empty spaciousness. She began "shaking like a leaf"; she could not get her bags through customs

without constant help; she had an impulse to tell everyone around who she was in case she went mad.

Ethel's problem continued and she became worried, although not
depressed. Her husband found it difficult to cope with her illness,
however, and became increasingly distant from her. Finally, he asked
for a divorce. With this, Ethel did become depressed, crying excessive-
ly and losing sleep and appetite. She also felt abandoned and entirely
alone.

OBSESSIVE PHOBIC COMPLICATIONS

Some agoraphobic people have even more than dread and depression
to worry about. They also suffer from what doctors refer to as *obsessive
phobias. Obsessions* are persistent thoughts that seem senseless, yet
the victim cannot make them stop. In the case of phobias, a person
typically suffers from extremely irrational doubts or dread. These often
include a fear of being contaminated or of losing control of oneself.
For example, a person may fear committing violence against him- or
herself or other people. Such a person becomes obsessed with the idea
that touching or even seeing a certain object might lead to a tragic
strangling, stabbing, shooting, or other act of mayhem.

In the vast majority of obsessive phobic cases, such violent acts
never actually occur. Nevertheless, the victim sincerely believes that
they might happen and is constantly frightened and distressed at the

*Obsessive phobias
occur in extreme
cases, when a person
has uncontrollable
thoughts that often
center on committing
violent acts. James
Ensor depicts ines-
capable notions in his
1895 illustration*
Demons Me Turlupinant
(Demons Tormenting
Me).

possibility. He or she might even contemplate committing suicide in order to escape the misery of living with such severe agoraphobia (although most cases of agoraphobia do not involve suicidal thoughts). In Zane's *Your Phobia*, a former steel worker recounted his ordeal:

> I have had a shotgun ever since I was a teenager. . . . All of a sudden, it became a frightening weapon. I was afraid I might take it and shoot one of my two boys or my wife. I can't be in a room alone with a sharp knife. I'm afraid I might take it and stab somebody. I'm becoming more and more depressed and now I'm afraid I might lose control and kill my whole family, then commit suicide. . . . This thing has become so frightening and upsetting, I think I'm going to go crazy; I've even thought about putting the muzzle of the shotgun in my mouth and blowing my brains out.

Although most agoraphobes do not obsess to this degree, it is not difficult to see why doctors look upon agoraphobia as a serious and potentially destructive disorder. The condition affects the way the subject acts, thinks, and feels. It often takes control of a person's entire life, forcing family and friends to adjust. For those who do not seek help, agoraphobia is a frightening and disabling condition that traps them in a self-made prison from which, they believe, it is impossible to escape.

Fortunately, relatively few people suffer from agoraphobia: One study estimates that it appears in approximately 1 of every 160 adults. Various studies report that between one-half to two-thirds of all agoraphobes are women, something experts are still unable to explain. However, one theory suggests that the disorder actually occurs equally among men and women, but because women may be more willing to seek professional help, their cases are reported more often.

Even among phobic people, agoraphobia is rare. Most phobics have only one particular phobia to confront. Yet even a single phobia can produce a great deal of anxiety, discomfort, and unhappiness, as the next chapter will demonstrate.

CHAPTER 4
PHOBIAS INVOLVING PLACES AND OBJECTS

Simple phobias are those that are stimulated by a single object or situation. They may involve something as small as a doll or a skein of yarn or as large as an airport or a bridge.

Simple phobias are those in which fear is stimulated by a single situation, activity, or object. (Animal fears are often placed in this category, but the next chapter will examine them more closely.) Because it is possible to identify in each of these cases the specific thing that triggers the phobic reaction, simple phobias are also referred to as *specific phobias*.

Even objects and situations that most people find tame and inoffensive can cause unreasoned fear in some people. Phobias of seemingly

Perched near the top of the Empire State Building, these workers over-look Manhattan without a hint of fear. For an acrophobe, a person who fears heights, this feat seems impossible.

harmless objects include balloons, buttons, books, letters, dolls, fuzzy objects, string, and even homemade cakes and pastries.

Although such fears of everyday objects exist, they affect only a small number of people. Most phobic reactions fall into more common categories that include far larger numbers of people. These are the most familiar phobias, the ones well known to every country, culture, racial group, and gender.

FEAR OF HEIGHTS

Everyone is cautious when standing near the unprotected edge of a high balcony or cliff. Falling is unlikely, though possible, so the average person is careful to avoid getting too near the edge. This caution is both natural and healthy.

Yet for someone who suffers from *acrophobia*, the fear of heights, the impulse for caution rises to a sensation of terror. The acrophobe experiences a very real feeling that he or she will fall. This fear persists even when a railing, fence, window, or other protective barrier is present. As long as the acrophobic person can see over the edge of the precipice, he or she is gripped by fright and panic.

The acrophobe may visualize his or her body plummeting downward. Sometimes he or she even feels a compulsion to jump, perhaps as a way, albeit an irrational one, to escape the feeling of dread. Even when the person reasons it out, thinking over and over, It's perfectly safe and I'm not going to fall, the fear is too strong. The individual reacts by fleeing the situation, moving far from the edge or back down to ground level.

Surprisingly, however, many acrophobes are not afraid to fly. Most acrophobic persons report that the dread is triggered by standing on structures connected to the ground—cliffs, buildings, or bridges, for example. On the other hand, some acrophobes do fear being in airplanes. This aspect of their condition may appear suddenly, even in the case of an experienced pilot. For instance, George T., a 55-year-old commercial pilot, had flown many different types of planes before he encountered the problem:

> It makes me angry just to think about it. I was flying along at about 4,000 feet, and everything seemed fine. Suddenly, I had the feeling my stomach had turned upside down. My heart started going a mile a minute. I thought at first maybe it was severe indigestion or something, but it wasn't. I just knew I had to get the plane down and myself on firm ground. Somehow I managed to land in one piece. Not only have I never gone up in another plane, but I'm even queasy when I'm in a tall building. I just can't understand it.

Crossing high bridges is a common dread among acrophobes. Many report that when they drive over a bridge, they fear looking from side to side and must concentrate on the center of the road in order to make it across the span without panicking. A few people actually "freeze" and stop their cars on the bridge. On some of the larger bridges, such as the George Washington Bridge in New York City, the police routinely patrol to help drivers who are too terrified to move any further.

Extreme acrophobes may visualize being trapped in their cars and hurtling over the edge of the bridge and crashing into the water. One journalist who suffers from fear of heights said that once when he drove over a bridge, he imagined the newspaper headline, AUTO DIVES OFF BRIDGE. DRIVER DROWNS. In his mind, this man considered what he dreaded to be possible, even probable.

Often, acrophobia is so severe that it can adversely affect an individual's work. In *Personality Development and Psychopathology*, Cameron and Rychlak report the case of Agnes W., a secretary in her thirties, who faced sudden terror one evening while she was working late. She was alone in her eighth-floor office when she became afraid that she would jump or fall from the open window. At first she was so terrified that all she could do was crouch near a file cabinet until she trusted herself to get out of the building. She suffered acute anxiety symptoms such as perspiration, pounding heart, and shortness of breath. It became impossible to return to work, and after two months she gave up her job. She eventually found a lesser-paying position in a store.

People who experience claustrophobia, the fear of enclosed spaces, may feel so trapped that they become frantic in their urge to escape. This predicament typically occurs in elevators but may also occur in tunnels, trains, theaters, and barber's chairs.

FEAR OF ENCLOSED PLACES

Another extremely common phobia is *claustrophobia*, the fear of being trapped in enclosed spaces. Sufferers typically feel unable to breathe and feel that they will suffocate if they cannot get outside to some fresh air. This reaction is similar to that of an acrophobe, wherein the victim feels he or she must immediately escape the situation or suffer injury or death.

Some researchers speculate that claustrophobia is due, at least to some degree, to *instinct*—the unconscious, inborn tendency to respond to specific stimuli in certain ways. Animals with healthy instincts are attracted to safe food and environments and avoid potentially dangerous situations. For instance, a wild animal trapped in an enclosed space usually becomes frantic, seeking any possible way to escape. Claustrophobic people react the same way, especially when the enclosed area is small or escape routes are blocked.

Elevators are the most common setting for claustrophobic reactions. Many claustrophobes say that they fear a power failure will occur, leaving them trapped between floors. The rational explanation that within a few minutes someone will arrive with help does not erase the victim's feelings of all-consuming dread. A person who fears elevators, for example, might compare the experience to being locked in a box and being unable to move his or her legs and arms or to get enough air.

To someone who is claustrophobic, elevators are only one example of "boxes," places sealed off from the outside world. Modes of transportation, such as cars, trains, subways, and buses, are also types of boxes in which claustrophobes become frightened. Some sufferers simply refuse to ride in these vehicles, expressing fears that they will faint, have a heart attack, or be unable to get out. Other claustrophobes complain about feeling trapped in churches, movie theaters, concert halls, or restaurants, especially if these places are crowded.

Another claustrophobic situation is the "chair"; for instance, barber, hairdresser, or dentist chairs can trigger an attack of claustrophobia. Even though the only thing holding a person in a barber's chair is a cloth or plastic sheet, the claustrophobe may grow increasingly alarmed and imagine that if he or she does not leap up immediately, escape will become impossible.

Like other phobics, claustrophobic individuals are often worried about what other people think of their strange behavior. This only serves to put them under more stress and worsen their symptoms of anxiety and panic. In *Personality Development and Psychopathology*, Cameron and Rychlak recount the case of Kenneth E., whose claustrophobic terror was intensified by knowing that people were watching his display of fear:

> The onset of his claustrophobic symptoms followed an acute anxiety attack in a theater. . . . When this occurred he became still more frightened that people around him in the theater would notice his agitation and guess its cause. As soon as the curtain fell for the intermission he staggered out, feeling weak, tremulous, and nauseated. After this, he could go to the theater only if he sat near an exit, and even then he felt so anxious that he lost all pleasure in being there. The phobia generalized to [other] places where he was thrown with strangers under crowded conditions.

Eventually, Kenneth's problem became so disabling that he sought professional help and decided to undergo therapy.

FEAR OF WATER

The phobia of water, called *hydrophobia*, is especially disabling, since water is so common in nature and also so important to the maintenance of life. Hydrophobia takes many forms. One type can be set off by moisture in the form of fog, mist, or even steam coming out of a kettle. By contrast, pouring water may trigger a phobic reaction in another hydrophobe. In *Your Phobia*, Zane describes one hydrophobe who has no problem looking at a lake or ocean but cannot endure seeing water come out of a spigot or a shower. This prevents the person from doing any cooking and requires that someone else fill the bathtub. The individual also reports fearing fountains and even water trickling down from a spring.

Hydrophobia, the fear of water, includes a wide range of terrors. Some people are afraid of vast bodies of water, whereas others fear flowing water; still others dread immersion in water for fear they will drown.

For other hydrophobes, being around large bodies of water creates a feeling of dread. Zane describes one man with this fear who will not go within miles of a lake or river and is especially fearful of the ocean. If he goes driving, he first gets a detailed topographical map so he can avoid any lake or river. He will not even go to a movie unless someone who has seen it assures him that it shows no bodies of water. Nor will he watch any television programs that have boats in them because they might also show water.

Another form of hydrophobia involves actually being immersed in water. Some victims of this phobia will not even climb into a bathtub. Sufferers who are comfortable swimming in shallow water will not wade out to water over their head because they are convinced that they will drown.

One bad experience involving water may lead a person to react fearfully in many other situations where water is present. Ellen P. describes how her problem began and intensified:

My boyfriend and I were out on his speedboat when the weather started to change. We couldn't get back to the marina before the storm hit, and we turned over. We were in the water for almost an hour [while] big waves kept washing over us. We made it back all right, but I was really terrified. Needless to say, I wouldn't go out on a boat again. Then one day we were fishing off the edge of a bridge and I had a sudden feeling that I was going to fall in the water, that the waves would come and the current would suck me under. My heart pounded in my chest, and I couldn't seem to catch my breath. I just told my boyfriend, "Get me out of here!" But that wasn't the end of it. Pretty soon every time I drove by the ocean, or even a lake, or went over a bridge that was above water, the feeling of terror and death would return. Before this happened, I never appreciated or understood what a friend of mine who suffers from anxiety goes through, but now I do.

OTHER SIMPLE PHOBIAS

There are several other common simple phobias, one typical example being hematophobia, the fear of blood. Most people are bothered by seeing someone bleed, yet they do not have an actual phobia of blood. Instead, when they see blood they exhibit a simple *aversion reaction*, such as looking away or making a face. The sentence "I can't stand the sight of blood" is common in many cultures because people associate the spilling of blood with death. Many people prefer not to watch blood being drawn from their own arms or to see it on meat in a butcher shop.

Some people, however, react much more strongly to the sight of blood. These are true hematophobes. In *Your Phobia*, Zane describes Tony B., who often faints when he sees blood on a person. At first a pinprick or a scratch showing the smallest amount of blood could set off panic in Tony. As time passed, Tony could not stand the sight of razors, knives, or any sharp objects. Eventually he gave up watching movies and television shows because he dreaded the possibility of seeing violence and gore.

Just as most hematophobes associate blood with death or pain, some women have an intense fear of childbirth because of the pain involved.

Gender Differences In Phobias*
Ranking by Prevalence of Individual Phobia by Sex

Rank F	Rank M	Phobia	Prevalence F	Prevalence M	Ratio F : M
1	2	Spiders, bugs, mice, snakes	6.63	2.44	2.7:1
2	1	Heights	4.57	3.16	1.4:1
3	5	Being on any public transportation (e.g., buses, airplanes, or elevators)	3.80	1.33	2.9:1
4	6	Being in water (e.g., a swimming pool or lake)	3.58	1.28	2.8:1
5	11	Storms	2.95	0.83	3.6:1
6	3	Being in a crowd	2.79	1.45	1.9:1
7	4	Other fears	2.70	1.36	2.0:1
8	8	Being in a closed place	2.67	1.36	2.0:1
9	10	Tunnels or bridges	2.34	0.86	2.7:1
10	9	Speaking in front of a small group of people one knows	1.92	1.11	1.7:1
11	14	Going out of the house alone	1.88	0.39	4.8:1
12	13	Being alone	1.68	0.43	3.9:1
13	15	Being near any harmless or dangerous animal even when out of reach	1.42	0.33	4.3:1
14	7	Speaking to strangers or meeting new people	1.32	1.20	1.1:1
15	12	Eating in front of other people	0.84	0.66	1.3:1

*Results of the Epidemiologic Catchment Area Program (ECA) Community Study, National Institute of Mental Health

These 1988 statistics show the differences between the things that men and women fear. Although phobias are documented in women more often than in men, experts suggest that men have an equal number of fears but are less willing to discuss them.

Those who suffer from *tocophobia*, the fear of childbirth, usually escape the fear by avoiding pregnancy in the first place. Some who become pregnant may even have abortions rather than undergo the birth process, which they are convinced they will not survive.

The fear of death is also linked to *tachophobia*, the fear of speed. Individuals with this phobia may feel perfectly safe driving their cars at 40 or 50 miles per hour, yet become gripped by sudden panic and a sense of impending doom when they reach 55 or 60 miles per hour, or some other arbitrary speed.

The situation is similar for those with aviophobia, the fear of flying. Statistically, accidents are more likely to occur in a car than in an airplane, yet this fact does not eliminate an aviophobe's dread.

HELPLESSNESS

The feeling of helplessness is a common factor in most phobias. Phobic people often believe that they are completely at the mercy of someone or something outside themselves. For example, a victim of *gymnophobia*, the fear of being naked, fears that if others see his or her nude body, they will savagely ridicule it.

People with *mysophobia*, the fear of dirt, feel they are at the mercy of an unsanitary world that will bring them disease and misery. They believe that the only way they can survive is to create an immaculate environment. Those suffering from *spefophobia*, the fear of germs, feel even more helpless because they cannot even see what they fear most. The situation is similar for people with *brontophobia*, an intense fear of thunder, since it too cannot be seen and strikes without warning.

So far, the discussion has centered on fears of inanimate objects and simple situations. Some people find things that are alive even more terrifying. They fear creatures that can move of their own accord and might chase their victims, hunt them down, jump on them, or crawl into their beds at night. The next chapter will examine phobias that are triggered by specific animals or animal traits.

A feeling shared by many phobic people is that of helplessness. For example, astraphobia, the fear of thunder and lightning, causes victims to feel that they are completely at the mercy of a power beyond their control.

CHAPTER 5

ANIMAL PHOBIAS

In this 1929 painting, Les Accomodations des Désirs, *Salvador Dalí expresses an anxious attitude toward animals. Zoophobia refers to the fear of animals, although most zoophobes fear one specific animal rather than all kinds.*

According to psychologists, most people experience some mild fear of spiders, bees, cats, snakes, or other animals at some time in their life. But unless these fears are intense enough to interfere with everyday life, they are not true phobias. However, people who do have phobic reactions to animals are among those whose fear "is one of the most common problems encountered by psychiatrists," according to Douglas Hunt in *No More Fears*.

Few people seem to be phobic toward all animals. The term *zoophobia* was coined in the late 1800s to describe this fear, but that label is rarely used today. Usually, a particular animal or group of animals is the object of dread. Hunt explains, "People who fall into this category usually complain of long-standing fears of a certain animal or insect but appear to be free of other symptoms. In other words, they don't fear all animals, only one species, and are usually quite comfortable with most forms of life, be they two-, four-, or eight-legged."

Most people who suffer from animal phobias insist that their problems began in childhood, usually before age eight. This coincides with early studies done by Sigmund Freud, the founder of *psychoanalysis*, a method of treating emotional disorders by encouraging the patient to discuss his or her feelings openly, especially those concerning early-childhood experiences and dreams. In 1913, Freud developed a theory of childhood animal phobias that included these ideas:

> The child suddenly begins to fear a certain animal species and to protect itself against seeing or touching

Many children express a fear of animals that they may have never encountered personally. These fears are often derived from fairy tales and legends, such as the story of St. Michael slaying the dragon, depicted in this 13th-century mural.

any individual of this species. . . . Sometimes animals which are known to the child only from picture books and fairy stories become objects of the senseless and inordinate anxiety which is manifest in these phobias.

Most people seem to outgrow these fears by their teenage years. A few do not, continuing to suffer even through adulthood. No one is sure why some people outgrow childhood fears of animals while others do not.

INSECTS AND OTHER CREATURES

Extreme fear of insects, or *entomophobia*, is one of the most common animal phobias. Although opinions differ as to exactly what it is about insects that causes such dread, their physical makeup and habits inspire

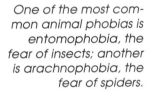

One of the most common animal phobias is entomophobia, the fear of insects; another is arachnophobia, the fear of spiders.

revulsion in many people. Insects have many legs, multiple eyes, and bodies that often end in stingers, features that many people consider repulsive and alien. In addition, some species live in filth, hide in dark holes, suck blood, or carry disease.

Though most people consider these traits and behaviors unappealing, entomophobes see them as horrifying. They vividly picture each part of the insect as a threat: the barbs on its legs, its wicked-looking mouth and eyes, and its feelers that vibrate. Such a person can feel so terrified that he or she becomes paralyzed in the presence of an insect.

Bees are commonly objects of phobic dread. The term *apiphobia*, the fear of bees, also includes wasps, flying ants, and other bee relatives. Although the possibility of being stung no doubt inspires some amount of fear, most of those who are terrified of bees report that it is the buzzing, swooping, and other menacing behaviors that cause the most apprehension.

Like other phobias, the fear of bees can occasionally become so overpowering that the victim's entire life is affected. For example, John D.'s bee phobia grew particularly debilitating. He recalled:

> I never did care much for bees, but I didn't know how much they actually bothered me until about three years ago, when they changed my whole life. The first incident was when two large yellow jackets came into the house through a light fixture. I saw them crawling around on the kitchen counter, and something inside me just snapped. I had to get out of the house. I'm sorry to admit that it was my wife that killed them. Then we found out that the nest was up in the attic, and even after the exterminator came, I wouldn't go upstairs anymore. When a nest started in the garage, I wouldn't go in there, either. Now I'm afraid to go out at all because the bees might be anywhere.

A variation on entomophobia is the fear of spiders. Of course, spiders are not insects, but many people tend to lump the two groups together, along with centipedes and other multilegged creatures. Nevertheless, experts actually use the term *arachnophobia* to differentiate the extreme fear of spiders from that of insects.

Those who suffer from arachnophobia often describe the creatures as sinister or evil, endowing spiders with a humanlike cunning that they certainly do not possess. Some psychiatrists suggest that such associations come from traditional children's stories in which spiders are pictured as having a cruel and destructive intelligence. The complicated webs that spiders spin to trap other creatures reinforce this image, and arachnophobes frequently identify with a spider's helpless prey.

BIRDS

Most people perceive birds as harmless creatures that wake them in the morning with pleasant songs or flutter gracefully overhead. However,

This movie still may depict the worst nightmare of an ornithophobe, a person who fears birds. In this 1907 film, Rescued from the Eagle's Nest, *an eagle kidnaps a helpless child.*

Hollywood's Favorite Foe— Animals

Since the earliest days of the movies, filmmakers have taken advantage of people's fears of certain animals. The 1981 adventure film *Raiders of the Lost Ark* depicts hero Indiana Jones admitting that he has "a thing" about snakes, meaning he has a phobic dread. Naturally, Jones is later forced to confront his fear. He must descend into a pit lined with thousands of snakes, a slithering mass of reptilian horror that has audiences squirming almost as much as the character.

Many early classic horror films also exploit the ancient fear of becoming inhuman animals. The fear of the beast within everyone is the subject of various versions of *Dr. Jekyll and Mr. Hyde*, which debuted as a film in 1931. In the original story by Robert Louis Stevenson, a scientist invents a formula that transforms him into a person with primitive, brutal traits. Hollywood has since exaggerated the idea, depicting Mr. Hyde as a monstrous creature.

Similar terrifying transformations of humans into wild animals have occurred in *Werewolf of London* (1935), *The Wolf Man*
(1940), *Cat People* (1942, 1982), and *The Ape Man* (1943). The legend of vampires that can turn themselves into wolves and bats has been exploited time and again on film.

Other films have featured animals that were especially large or particularly cunning. In the classic *King Kong* (1933), the giant ape set the standard for abnormally large animal attackers. *Willard* (1971) and *Ben* (1972) are movies about clever rats who lead an army of rodents in revenge against humans. The huge and especially smart killer shark in *Jaws* (1975) still makes beachgoers think twice before taking a dip in the ocean. Even man's best friend goes wrong in *Cujo* (1983), the tale of a rabid dog who kills his owner and traps a terrified woman and child in a car.

Beginning in the 1950s, insects became a popular Hollywood scare tactic, and crawling creatures still threaten audiences today. A recent example is *Arachnophobia*, a 1990 movie about scientists who unwittingly unleash an especially lethal type of spider in rural America. In the

Over the years, Hollywood has used the fear of animals to produce innumerable horror films. Some are silly, but others, such as Werewolf of London, *are classics that have captured the imaginations of late-night TV watchers for decades.*

climactic scene, the hero, who suffers from a classic spider phobia, must overcome his fear or die. To make the audience as uncomfortable as possible, the camera continually shows close-ups of hideous spiders crawling over the actors' bodies.

One variation of insect thrillers uses vermin of gigantic size, a sickening reversal of roles in which bugs try to squash people. Examples include a praying mantis in *The Deadly Mantis* (1957) and a moth in *Mothra* (1962). Another approach shows bugs attacking in vast swarms. The world has been repeatedly threatened by ants (*Them!* [1954]), bees (*The Swarm* [1978], *The Killer Bees* [1974]), grasshoppers (*The Beginning of the End* [1957]), scorpions (*The*

Black Scorpion [1957]), and spiders, both singularly (*Tarantula* [1955]) and en masse (*Kingdom of the Spiders* [1977]).

Perhaps no one has filmed an animal assault on humans better than director Alfred Hitchcock in *The Birds* (1963). Because most people think of birds as harmless creatures, their mass attacks on people in a small American town make this movie all the more bizarre. This illogical story demonstrates the thoughts of a phobic person taken to extremes: A harmless creature becomes an object of all-consuming dread. Yet most creatures do not deserve such negative stereotypes. They are inclined to avoid humans altogether, unless they get wind of a tasty picnic and invite themselves over for a snack.

to those suffering from *ornithophobia*, birds are objects of horror. These people describe "beating wings," "wicked beak and claws," and "fluttering and swooping about" as the most frightening aspects of the creatures.

Oddly enough, eagles, hawks, and other large birds of prey are not the birds that typically terrify ornithophobes. Instead, pigeons are most often cited as triggering phobic reactions. Other docile, seemingly harmless birds also cause phobic reactions, including chickens.

For some people, the terror extends even to feathers. In *Your Phobia*, Zane describes a woman in her sixties who remembers how a hen pecked at her face when she was a child. After that, the sight of a feather sent her into hysterics. Another woman had a dread of feathers and refused to keep feather pillows in her home. She could not even tolerate the thought of putting her head on a feather or down pillow.

CATS AND DOGS

Since ancient times, people have viewed cats with awe and fear. These creatures, which have occupied a prominent place in human myths and fables, are often portrayed as sinister and evil. For example, witches are depicted as having feline companions or transforming themselves into cats. Many superstitions are built around cats, especially black cats, as omens of impending death or disaster.

Yet it is not these myths that people suffering from *ailurophobia*, the fear of cats, find terrifying. Instead they fear the eyes and fur and the possibility that a cat might rub up against them. When visiting friends who have cats, they often ask that the animals be locked up and kept out of sight.

Anita N. recalled an incident that occurred as she approached her car in a mall parking lot. Suddenly, she noticed a large cat staring at her from another car. She panicked and, no matter how many times she told herself that the cat could not open the car windows and reach her, she could not calm down. In fact, she was so upset that she refused to drive past the car with the cat in it and had to call her husband to come get her. After a while, she was afraid to go anywhere in public for fear she might encounter a cat. So she retreated to her home, the only place

Many myths associate cats with dark powers, often matching them with the evil deeds of witches. Yet the majority of ailurophobes, people who dread cats, actually fear the animal's eyes and fur most.

where she felt safe. This sequence of events illustrates how a simple fear may grow into a full-blown phobia, in which the person isolates him- or herself from the rest of the world.

Cynophobia, the fear of dogs, is not nearly as widespread as the fear of cats, perhaps because dogs are often perceived as "man's best friend" and tend to be more affectionate than cats. When most people think of dogs, they picture cuddly puppies or kindly beasts obeying their master's bidding. Nevertheless, some people are phobic about dogs. Often, as seems to be the case with many animal phobias, this dread is triggered by memories of a frightening childhood experience.

REPTILES

Snakes and other reptiles have long been associated with evil and mischief. The myths and legends of all races include fearsome dragons or other giant reptilian beasts as well as snakes that display a human-like and evil intelligence. The Old Testament tale about the snake tempting Eve is only one example.

The human aversion to reptiles may be a primitive, ingrained fear. In his book *The Dragons of Eden*, renowned scientist Dr. Carl Sagan proposed that people's fear of reptiles is an instinctual memory. According to this view, primitive mammalian ancestors once existed in a world dominated by dinosaurs and other large reptiles. The mammals' desire to escape these huge beasts was stored in mammalian brains as a survival instinct and remains there today, although the largest reptiles have long been extinct. Although there is no way to test this theory, the idea may help explain where some animal phobias originated.

The physical attributes of reptiles continue to instill fear in people today, perhaps because they are scaly and have sharp teeth or fangs.

One theory suggests that the fear of reptiles is due to an inborn tendency among humankind's primitive mammal ancestors to avoid dinosaurs.

They are also cold-blooded, which gives them an unfeeling, alien quality that sets them apart from warm-blooded birds and mammals, and some reptiles are actually poisonous. Even so, experts are not certain that these factors are the ones that cause *herpetophobia*, the fear of reptiles.

In the most common variant of the condition, *ophidiophobia*, the fear of snakes, the speed and cunning of the creatures seems to evoke the most terror. Typical fears include snakes "slithering up on you" or "coiling around you" or "the slimy feeling of their skin." Few people with this problem have actually had physical contact with a snake, yet even seeing a picture of a snake may be enough to bring on symptoms of extreme anxiety.

INDIRECT ANIMAL PHOBIAS

In addition to phobias of specific animals, there are fears that are only indirectly connected to living things. For instance, *cnidophobia*, the fear of being stung, does not relate to any one animal, but might be applied to bees, wasps, spiders, snakes, lizards, and other creatures. Similarly, someone with *odontophobia*, the fear of teeth, can be frightened by any animal with fairly large or prominent teeth, even when that person is not afraid of that specific type of animal.

Since many animals carry rabies, people suffering from *lyssophobia*, the fear of getting rabies, often try to avoid all animals to keep from contracting the disease. Those with *coprophobia*, the fear of feces, may stay away from animals because of the danger of coming into contact with their droppings. People with *doraphobia*, the fear of fur, cannot stand to be around furry creatures, whereas those with *parasitophobia*, the fear of parasites, avoid most animals, even when the creatures are not known to carry parasites.

One factor that makes animal and other related phobias so hard for sufferers to control is that animals are practically everywhere. They are pets in people's homes, wild creatures inhabiting woods, fields, lakes, and oceans, and subjects in movies, television programs, and magazine ads. Sooner or later, the phobic person is bound to encounter the thing he or she dreads.

The situation is even worse for individuals who suffer from phobias involving other human beings. Other than becoming a hermit, there is no way to avoid coming into contact with other people. These crippling fears will be considered in the following chapter.

CHAPTER 6

PHOBIAS INVOLVING PEOPLE

The painting Le Faux Miroir *(The False Mirror) by René Magritte (1898–1967) suggests the greatest fear affecting those with phobias of people—that others are watching and judging them.*

Phobias that have to do with people are often referred to as social phobias. Many people who suffer from these phobias are overly concerned with what others think of them. As a result, the image they wish to project to others is strongly affected by their intense need to be liked. Although just about everyone wants to look good and gain the admiration of peers or the public at large, a socially phobic person worries about appearing worthless and incompetent if he or she does not achieve these goals.

This fear may eventually inspire avoidance behavior. For instance, a person who believes that he or she is ugly or hopelessly unattractive may begin to shun appearing in public. By the same token, individuals who are convinced that their personality is lacking or that they are not forceful enough when meeting others might avoid contact with people whenever possible.

Such fears are also related to the anxiety that often occurs when students sit down to take an examination. Psychologists frequently work with patients suffering from test anxiety, so the phenomenon has been extensively studied. If the test is of minor importance and unlikely to affect the student's grades, he or she usually suffers little or no anxiety. However, if the test is an important one, which could affect the student's standings and future opportunities, he or she may experience what seems like overwhelming anxiety.

For some sufferers of test anxiety, this reaction is so intense that it negatively affects their test scores as well as their self-esteem. Such anxiety is due not only to the fear of failure but also to the fear of what others will think of that failure.

Test anxiety affects students who, though they may have spent many hours in preparation, become fearful when presented with an important test. Such students are often preoccupied with concerns of what others may think if they fail.

Most of the people at the 1985 Live Aid concert enjoyed this major social event. Yet even fun events make many people feel somewhat shy at first. On the other hand, those with true social phobias are so apprehensive that they cannot socialize normally.

ARE SOCIAL PHOBIAS REALLY PHOBIAS?

Although the word *phobia* is used to describe many of these social anxieties, some experts say that this categorization may not be scientifically accurate. They insist that in many of these cases it is difficult to tell when someone has crossed the line from normal to truly phobic behavior.

Shyness is one example of a normal social fear. Most people display some degree of shyness at one time or another, depending on the situation. In *No More Fears*, Hunt claims, "There is a normal social anxiety that all of us experience. Who isn't just a bit shy on occasion; who doesn't have trouble saying no to [inconvenient] requests? Who among us is not anxious, if only a little, when he must speak to an audience?"

Yet some people are so shy that they cannot function normally in everyday life. As one subject explained to Hunt:

> I always imagined people were critical of me. I worried what they thought about me. These fears filled me with

a lack of self-confidence. My head was always down, and my shoulders were slumped. I could never look anyone straight in the eye. If I saw someone I knew coming along the street, I would cross to the other side so I wouldn't have to speak as I passed. [Being in] a roomful of people would throw me into a panic, and I would leave quickly. I even hesitated [before] answering the phone. You'll never know how lonely and depressed I felt.

Because each person is different, a fear that may allow one person to continue functioning normally may cause a complete inability to function in someone else. The extent to which these fears affect a person's life determines whether or not he or she suffers from a true phobia.

FEAR OF THE DENTIST

Anxiety about visiting the dentist is a common fear in modern society. Reasons for such apprehension vary from person to person. Whereas one individual may be afraid of the threat of pain, another may fear the possibility that he or she will bleed. Some people interpret the dentist's probings inside the mouth as an invasion of the private inner space of their body. Whatever the reasons, dentists say that a majority of people exhibit some amount of anxiety about dental visits.

In contrast to these normal displays of anxiety, some individuals show extreme phobic reactions toward a visit to the dentist.

The characteristic symptoms of a panic attack, including pounding heart, trembling limbs, and heavy perspiration, may occur during a routine session with the dentist. How many people have such a problem? A 1989 report estimated that 150 million Americans fear going to the dentist, while 25 million suffer from dental phobias so severe that they refuse to go.

For victims who are so fearful that after one or two terror-filled experiences early in life they never visit the dentist again, this problem is especially serious. Rather than return, they may allow their teeth to decay, which in turn causes pain and other social and job-related

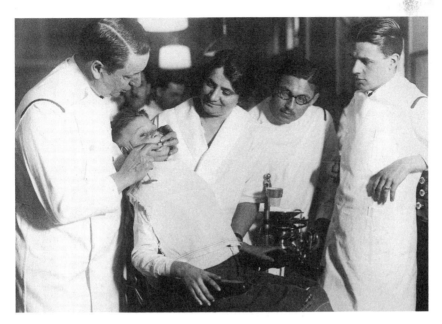

Dentists report that most people display some degree of anxiety during a typical visit. Yet it is estimated that 25 million Americans suffer from such severe dental phobia that they refuse to have their teeth examined at all.

problems. In his book *Cure and Care of Neuroses*, Isaac Marks describes the case of a shipping clerk in his twenties:

> At age seven he was taken to the dentist by his mother; he panicked and was virtually forced into the dental chair. . . . His last visit to a dentist was when he was 11 years old. Between age 13 and 14 he noticed that his teeth were decaying and began to brush them twice daily for 15 minutes and use a mouthwash regularly. As decay increased, he used homemade fillings. . . . He suffered from sharp-edged teeth, dental abscesses, and ulcerated gums. He became embarrassed by his toothache, unsightly teeth, and bad breath. This severely restricted his social life. To improve his appearance before his rare ventures from home, he painted his teeth white. He wished to change his job but could not face an interview due to his unsightly teeth.

Psychologists point out that it is important that dentists be careful not to reinforce the negative myths and stereotypes about dental visits. Although even the kindest of dentists cannot rid a patient of a dental phobia, a rough or callous dentist can easily increase a person's fears.

Fear on the Other Side of the Chair

Although fear of going to the dentist is well known, few people are aware that there is actually a phobia of practicing dentistry. Yet the condition is not all that rare. Hundreds of such cases are reported to psychiatrists each year.

According to experts, there may be several different reasons why dentists develop such fears. One possibility is that the dentist works so hard for so long that he or she becomes vulnerable to stress and job burnout. Or perhaps the dentist unsuccessfully performs a difficult procedure that causes a patient extreme pain or injury. The dentist, believing that the same thing might happen again, then fears working on another patient.

In one reported case, a young man wanted to be a surgeon, but his father was a dentist and expected him to enter the same profession. Later, after the young man began practicing dentistry, his office burned down. Although he had it rebuilt and continued with his practice, he began to show increasing symptoms of anxiety. He tried quitting the profession but felt he was running away from his troubles and resumed his practice. During his time away, the symptoms of his phobia had disappeared, but when he returned they grew worse than ever, until he eventually went into therapy. The existence of such cases illustrates that highly trained medical personnel are just as susceptible to disabling anxiety and phobias as anyone else.

FEAR OF PUBLIC SPEAKING

The fear of speaking in front of an audience is widespread in every modern culture. The apprehension is not confined to making formal speeches but also affects people in related situations. For instance,

Although some people thoroughly enjoy being in the spotlight, phonophobes dread public speaking to such a degree that they suffer panic attacks.

students standing before their classmates or executives presenting information at company meetings often exhibit clear-cut symptoms of anxiety.

Although a case of the jitters, even a bad one, is common when facing an audience, some people have actual panic attacks when placed in the public spotlight. The clinical term for the condition is *phonophobia*, the dread of public speaking. For example, Alan J., a salesman, explained that he had no difficulty at all when talking to people one-on-one and considered himself effective at his job. But when he was asked to give a speech at a regional company convention,

> that was a whole different story. I knew about the
> speech for weeks in advance. I kept telling myself that

it would be no problem. But then the day came. I was sitting at my table and my boss was introducing me. All of a sudden, I felt like I wasn't getting enough oxygen. I looked at the others—they were all right, so I knew it was just me. I knew I couldn't get up there in front of everybody; they would think I was no good. I would never work again. My legs were weak, and I could feel my heart thumping away. Everybody started clapping for me. I stood up somehow, and that was the last thing I remember. Later they said I fainted.

As often happens in cases of severe phobia, Alan's experience so frightened him that other areas of his life began to suffer. He lost a great deal of self-confidence, which adversely affected his sales work. Eventually, he went into therapy.

FEARING THOSE WHO ARE DIFFERENT

The fear and distrust of people who are physically, culturally, or behaviorally different is as old as humanity itself. The most familiar term associated with this is *xenophobia*, the fear of strangers or foreigners, which has affected people in all nations throughout history. It is debatable whether or not xenophobia is a true phobia.

Xenophobic fear is based, to a large degree, on a society's belief that people with strange customs, languages, and values will upset and destroy the traditional social structure. Yet history shows that change is both natural and inevitable. If new ideas and values do not come from the outside, they will eventually come from within. The changes brought about by these new ideas can be either positive or negative, depending on how the society responds. Often the society's fear of change is based on a cultural bias rather than a true phobia.

The fear of those who are different can also apply to those who represent a certain minority within an established society. Each culture has its own minorities, divided by factors such as national origin, skin color, or spiritual belief. Even today, members of such groups, termed *ethnic*, *racial*, and *religious* minorities, struggle to eliminate the prejudices and distrust that they encounter.

Homophobia

One minority that exists in every human society also crosses over traditional ethnic, racial, and religious lines. Referred to as *homosexuals*, members of the group are defined by having a sexual orientation toward members of their own sex.

The fear and hatred of homosexuals is a deep-rooted emotional reaction that appears in cultures around the world. People who are bothered by homosexuality may call it disgusting or outrageous, believing that it destroys social values. These people often accuse homosexuals of forcing their life-style on others who want nothing to do with it. Although these individuals have an irrational fear of homosexuality, called *homophobia*, it is unlikely that this is a true phobia.

Most experts argue that homophobia is not a true phobia because it does not involve a reaction against specific objects or situations. Rather, they suspect that homophobes fear homosexuality because they believe it to be unnatural—an opinion that seems based in misunderstanding. In the 1970s, the American Psychiatric Association took the stance that homosexuality is not unnatural, at least in the sense of contradicting natural law. This group of experts suggested that homosexuality is a *natural deviation*, a trait that occurs naturally among a small minority of people in every generation.

Regardless of whether xenophobia and homophobia express social intolerance or true phobias, the result is often the same: prejudice, a bias that can be detrimental to every individual within a minority as well as society in general.

INDIRECT SOCIAL PHOBIAS

Many social phobias stem from a specific source. Therefore, they are easy to deal with by using avoidance behavior. For instance, *necrophobia*, the fear of dead people, is easily controlled as long as the phobic person does not come into contact with a corpse—although in some cases, a photograph or movie depicting a dead body may trigger a phobic reaction. Another example is *coitophobia*, the dread of sexual intercourse. Because this act is generally voluntary, it can usually be avoided. One exception is rape, which may actually induce this phobia in some victims.

Over the years many different types of phobias have been reported to doctors, leading medical experts to devote a great deal of time and energy to the study of anxiety and phobias. Since the 19th century, doctors have looked long and hard for treatments while trying to understand the reasons behind these strange and severe conditions. Some theories on possible causes will be explored in the next chapter.

CHAPTER 7

CAUSES OF ANXIETY AND PHOBIAS

Many experts feel that anxiety is based on modeling, which occurs when a child watches his or her parents and responds as they do. If the child observes them acting fearful or insecure, he or she is likely to adopt the same behavior.

A number of theories proposed by psychologists and psychiatrists must be considered when explaining the causes of modern-day anxiety. Although each theory has adherents with a great deal of evidence to support their views, no single viewpoint has proved more valid than the others.

People who suffer from severe anxiety are almost constantly tense, uneasy, and worried. They frequently feel depressed and have trouble interacting with other people. They also tend to have difficulty making decisions and to feel apprehensive about life, no matter how well things seem to be going. The following theories suggest the cause of this painful condition.

CAUSES OF ANXIETY

Experts identify several factors involved in the development of anxiety. One is *modeling*, the idea that people learn to respond in certain ways by imitating the reactions of others. For example, a child who sees that a parent is fearful may become afraid, too. In fact, some studies have shown that most nervous, anxious children have nervous, anxious parents.

The Insecurity Factor

Studies also suggest that many parents who suffer from anxiety have unusually high expectations of their children. They demand that the youngsters perform as perfectly as possible, both in school and at home. Because the children cannot always live up to these strict standards, they become fearful and begin to show symptoms of anxiety. This condition can then plague them throughout their life.

In one case study reported in James Coleman's book *Abnormal Psychology and Modern Life*, a man in his thirties was suffering from such severe anxiety that he suspected he had heart trouble. In therapy he discovered that his problem began in childhood when:

> No matter what his accomplishments, his parents belittled and rejected him. When he once proudly told them that the school counselor had informed him he had a very high IQ, the parents demanded to know why he didn't make better grades. He remembered occasionally receiving presents, such as a model airplane set, that were always beyond his age level.

Anger and Anxiety

Another possible cause of anxiety is the subject's fear of being unable to control his or her impulses. These impulses are feelings that are actually normal, such as anger, hostility, and sexual desire. Yet the anxious person believes that these feelings are wrong, that he or she should not have them, and tries not to give in to them. But because these feelings are natural, they do not disappear; instead, the person has *repressed* them, buried them deep inside. The longer they are repressed, the more the feelings intensify and the more need the person has to release them. The unfortunate result of this constant inner conflict is a state of severe anxiety.

Painful Past Experiences

Memories of past painful situations can also increase anxiety. When faced with a stressful situation, a person may suddenly be reminded of an experience that was extremely traumatic or painful. Because the person relates the present experience with the past one, his or her previous feelings resurface, bringing renewed symptoms of anxiety.

One example of this condition, from *Personality Development and Psychopathology* by Cameron and Rychlak, is that of Walter A., a man in his thirties who was experiencing severe episodes of anxiety. These episodes always occurred at times when he was having difficulty in relationships with women. In therapy, it became clear that traumatic

One theory suggests that fears of natural occurrences developed in response to humankind's inability to understand such things. For example, early humans feared darkness and thunderstorms because they knew these things were dangerous but could not explain why they happened.

experiences from Walter's childhood were affecting the way he reacted to situations in his adult life. His parents had drummed into him at an early age that he must not sin; if he did, he would burn in hell.

Walter's parents had instilled in him the idea that marriage was the holiest union and that marriage vows should never be broken. But when Walter was 15, his mother suddenly divorced his father. This was very traumatic for Walter, who now saw his mother as a terrible sinner. He then deduced that all women were basically untrustworthy. Later, each time he began to get close to a woman, his past experience would haunt him, and his inability to cope triggered severe feelings of anxiety.

CAUSES OF PHOBIAS

The earliest human beings, hunter-gatherers who lived hundreds of thousands of years ago, probably experienced phobias. It is impossible to know for sure what these phobias were, but it stands to reason that people were frightened by the dangers they encountered most often—wild creatures and forces of nature.

Primitive humans developed instincts to fear these natural threats, and such fear then helped them avoid potentially dangerous situations. Early men and women probably reacted to these threats much as children do today—with extreme fear—because, like children, they could not explain many of the dangers they faced, such as the darkness of night and animal attacks. Interestingly, humankind's oldest phobias are now most common among its youngest members.

Even today, the most prevalent fears that affect small children are those that involve animals and nature. In *Cure and Care of Neuroses*, Marks explains, "Fears of animals are commonest at age two to four, but a couple of years later have been supplanted by fears of the dark and imaginary creatures."

The dark itself, and the dangers that often lurked within it, may have most filled humankind's earliest ancestors with dread. Today, doctors call extreme fear of the dark *achluophobia*. Although most adults are not phobic about nighttime, few can honestly say that walking through a dark forest is not somewhat unnerving. Perhaps there is a bit of the achluophobe in all people, an instinct left over from the days when death often hid in the darkness.

The Role of Displacement

Although instinct and evolution may contribute to the development of phobias, experts also believe that past traumatic experiences also play a major role. An individual may experience apprehension and dread when a seemingly unrelated and harmless object or situation reminds him or her of some earlier painful experience. Experts call this condition *displacement* because the person takes an ordinary object and indirectly replaces it with an image from a previous traumatic event.

This idea forms the basis of the psychoanalytic explanation of phobias, which was first proposed by Freud. In 1908, Freud examined the case of Little Hans, a five-year-old boy who was terrified that he might be bitten by horses.

After studying the case for some time, Freud concluded that Hans's phobia about horses was actually a displaced fear of his father. Supposedly, the boy was afraid of his father because he competed with Hans for the attention of the youngster's mother. According to Freud,

Sigmund Freud (1856–1939), founder of psychoanalysis, theorized that phobias are due to displacement, a condition that occurs when a person transfers fears of an earlier object or incident onto a more recent, often unrelated, substitute.

one part of Hans wanted his father to go away but another part wanted him to stay. This inner conflict caused the boy a great deal of guilt and frustration. It was too painful to face the fact that his father was the source of his fears, so Hans chose a symbol to represent his father, something on which to displace his fears—a horse. Of course, all of this was going on in Hans's *subconscious* mind, which means that he was not conscious, or aware, of these thoughts.

Freud applied this theory to all phobias, proposing that they are actually the result of displaced anxiety related to the mother-father-child relationship. Since Freud's day, however, many psychologists and psychiatrists have disagreed on whether this interpretation can be applied to all phobias. They point out that phobic reactions can result from many different kinds of stressful situations, not just those involving parents.

Conditioning for Phobias

Many experts believe that phobias are also influenced by *conditioning*. This view was first suggested by psychologist John B. Watson, who believed that fear, the basis of phobias, was a learned experience. He proposed that people are *conditioned* to feel fear, that is, they learn to

John Watson (1878–1958) was one of the first psychologists to offer evidence that phobias are due to conditioning—learning to associate new objects or situations with previous, often similar, subjects of dread.

associate certain objects and situations with similar things that have been scary or uncomfortable.

In 1920, Watson and Rosalie Rayner Watson conducted a now-famous experiment. In the tradition of Freud's "Little Hans," the Watsons' subject, an 11-month-old boy named Albert, became known as Little Albert. Originally, Albert enjoyed playing with a docile laboratory rat. Then, each time the child played with the animal, the Watsons banged steel bars loudly behind Albert's head. After this noise was repeated a few times, the child became afraid of the rat, even when they stopped making the noise when the rat appeared. Albert had learned to associate the rat with an unpleasant experience.

But the experiment did not end with the rat. In time, the researchers noticed that Albert also began to shun objects that were similar in appearance to the rat, including a rabbit, a skein of cotton wool, and the fur collar of a coat. They concluded that the child had been conditioned to fear furry objects. Although this study seemed to prove the theory, this sort of experiment would not be used today because it actually creates the fear that researchers are trying to prevent.

According to Zane, the conditioning theory might explain why phobic fears are so irrational. It seems that a phobic person may somehow connect many things to the original traumatic event. To illustrate this idea, Zane cites the case of a female college student who was riding in a car with her friends after a party. The road was icy, and the car reeled down an embankment and rolled over several times. Four of the teens were killed, and only the young woman survived. She remained trapped by the wreckage for hours while the car's radio kept playing rock music. Several weeks later, the girl suddenly began to dislike rock music. Her feelings intensified into a phobia, and eventually she could not tolerate hearing rock music at all, even at parties or dance clubs.

Modeling In Phobias

According to many doctors, modeling, the process by which a person learns by imitating others, also causes phobias. Researcher O. Hobart Mowrer used the example of chickens and chicken hawks to dem-

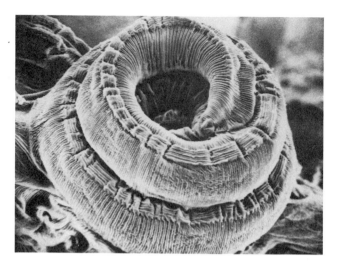

All living organisms respond to stress. For instance, this soil-dwelling organism, called a nematode, forms a tight coil when deprived of water. The human body has developed its own type of reactions to both physical and mental stress.

onstrate this idea. At first, he explained, baby chicks pay no particular attention to the shadow of a hawk flying overhead. The older chickens, however, begin to squawk loudly and raise a ruckus. After observing this behavior a number of times, the chicks also begin to squawk when the hawk's shadow appears. According to this theory, it is not necessary for the chicks to have a frightening experience with the hawk. They need only a certain behavior to imitate and they learn to panic.

People are as likely to learn the attitudes of others as are chickens. When trusted loved ones show irrationally fearful behavior, they teach those around them to be afraid. For instance, if parents become agitated at the sight of mice or dogs or dirt on the kitchen floor, two-year-old observers may learn to do the same, carrying this into their adult life.

THE BIOLOGY OF FEAR

Research indicates that anxiety displacement, conditioning, modeling, and repression of painful experiences are factors that affect anxiety and phobias. All of these explanations are psychological, relating to the mind and how it copes with the experiences of life. Yet science has revealed that the body's biochemical processes also seem to play a part in anxiety and phobic reactions.

One essential question that researchers consider is whether anxiety and phobias are hereditary—whether a person is born with a condition by inheriting it through the parent's *genes*. (Genes are the mechanisms that carry biological information determining specific physical traits.) Some evidence supports this idea, yet it is difficult to prove. Studies of identical twins (twins possessing an identical set of genes) find that both children have a similar susceptibilty to anxiety, whereas fraternal twins (twins whose genes differ somewhat) have varying tendencies toward anxiety. Anxiety is a difficult trait to measure, however, because environmental factors (such as where a person lives or how he or she is raised) also play a large role. None of the twins studied suffered from a full-fledged phobia.

Physiological Aspects

To understand the physical causes of anxiety, scientists have begun asking, "Which comes first? A mental awareness of the threat and then a physical panic reaction, or vice versa?" This question is especially important for those who suffer panic attacks. If a drug can be found to prevent the physical symptoms from occurring in the first place, the person may never begin to experience fear and the attack may never come.

To answer this question, researchers have studied the *sympathetic nervous system*. Part of the overall nervous system, the sympathetic nervous system takes over in an emergency situation, causing fear reactions that forewarn when disaster may strike. Under normal circumstances, these reactions help an individual escape danger: The pupils dilate to improve vision; the heart and breathing rates increase to pump more oxygen; blood moves to the muscles and brain, where it prepares the body to move and think faster; and sweat prepares to cool the muscles.

In studying these physiological changes, researchers have gained insight into the link between emotion and corresponding areas in the brain. In one experiment, scientists inserted electrodes into the brains of monkeys. Depending on where the electrode was placed, each

Scientists have found that patients with anxiety disorders overproduce a natural chemical called lactic acid during exercise. For most people, physical activity offers a healthy way to handle normal anxiety. (Pictured: record-breaking runner Marita Koch.)

monkey would respond with a different emotion. This suggests that specific emotions, including anxiety, are regulated in specific parts of the brain.

In addition, these experiments helped scientists discover that certain chemicals administered to particular areas of the brain create the same effect. Chemicals injected into the same brain areas where electrodes had been used produced the same emotional responses. Many of the chemicals used are produced within the body itself, suggesting that these chemicals work regularly to increase or decrease the intensity of emotional responses. Like other emotions, anxiety is affected by these chemical interactions in the brain.

Biochemical Functions

Other researchers have looked specifically at how the body functions. They have pinpointed certain areas that seem to malfunction in people with anxiety problems. Within the central nervous system there are *nerve endings*, which send chemical messages, and *receptors*, which receive these messages as they travel to the brain. Some researchers believe that the nerve endings in an overly anxious person are overactive, thus releasing an overabundance of the chemical *catecholamine*, one of the body's natural stimulants.

Meanwhile, a similar principle may also be acting in reverse when it comes to relief of anxiety. As with catecholamine, the body produces natural tranquilizers, called *inhibitory neurotransmitters*, to slow down the nerve endings in the central nervous system. Research suggests that in the body of an overly anxious person, these chemicals are not released properly and the person has difficulty calming down.

An important study at Massachusetts General Hospital in the 1940s revealed another substance that seems to have a clear impact on people

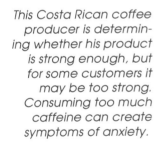

This Costa Rican coffee producer is determining whether his product is strong enough, but for some customers it may be too strong. Consuming too much caffeine can create symptoms of anxiety.

who already suffer from panic attacks. The study examined phobics whose anxiety seemed linked to exercise. When the subjects worked out for extensive periods their condition worsened. Researchers tested the patients' blood and discovered unusually high amounts of a substance called *lactic acid*, one of the by-products of muscle activity. This suggested that people who suffer from anxiety may be intolerant to lactic acid and may want to decrease their amount of exercise in order to reduce the flow of this substance.

In 1966, Dr. Ferris Pitts injected lactic acid into subjects who were known to suffer panic attacks, and it immediately produced symptoms of the attack. When he stopped the flow of lactic acid, the patients' symptoms ceased. Yet when Pitts injected subjects who were not prone to anxiety, they showed no physical change. Eventually, researchers discovered that adding calcium ions to the lactic acid helped reduce the severity of the anxiety.

Researchers are using the information they have gained about the body's natural chemicals to investigate possible treatments with drugs. However, scientists still have much to learn about the way in which the brain's chemicals work. Studies are further complicated by the interaction of many different chemicals and mechanisms within the brain.

Chemicals and Drugs

Research indicates that in addition to the body's own natural triggers, certain substances found in foods or drugs can also set off a panic attack. If consumed by certain people in sufficient amounts, substances such as caffeine, processed sugar, and even natural sugars (those found in honey or fruit) can cause problems. In the case of caffeine, one laboratory experiment showed that some people who had never before experienced panic suddenly did so after consuming eight cups of coffee in rapid succession. One possible reason for this is that caffeine upsets the body's calcium balance, a condition that can cause paniclike symptoms.

Alcohol, and drugs such as cocaine and amphetamines, can also trigger panic attacks. For example, when alcohol is ingested frequently, it can deplete the body's stores of vitamins and minerals, leading to

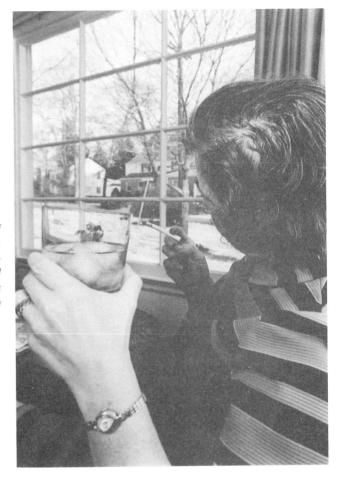

Alcohol can also trigger panic attacks, because it depletes the body's supply of vitamins and minerals. According to a study of 102 patients in clinics for the treatment of alcohol abuse, one-third of these individuals also suffered from severe phobias.

panic reactions. According to a 1979 study by J. A. Mullaney and C. J. Trippett in the *British Journal of Psychiatry*, one-third of the subjects they studied who were in clinics for treatment of alcohol abuse also suffered from disabling phobias. However, similar studies have shown much lower estimates, leaving the issue unresolved.

There are other triggers for anxiety and panic that come from the individual's environment. People with normal levels of anxiety do not seem to be affected by these external factors, but those individuals with anxiety disorders are likely to be more susceptible to them. These factors include fluorescent lights, which affect sensitive nerves in the eyes; industrial and household chemicals, which poison the body in a number of ways; and many foods that cause allergic reactions.

Considering all the different factors that appear to lead to anxiety and phobias, both psychological and physical, it is no wonder that so many millions of people suffer from such conditions. Luckily, there are treatments for these problems. The various ways that professionals deal with anxiety and phobias will be examined in the next chapter.

CHAPTER 8

TREATMENTS FOR ANXIETY AND PHOBIAS

Doctors have been trying to treat mental disorders for centuries. This circa-1600 engraving by Matthäus Greuter pictures a heat treatment for such problems.

Not all phobias require treatment. Some can be ignored as long as the dreaded object or situation is avoided. Others may disappear on their own after a period of time, depending on the type of phobia and the person's age when it first appears. Yet some anxiety disorders can be so disruptive to a person's life that the sufferer should seek treatment as soon as he or she recognizes that there is a problem.

Just as there are a number of different reasons behind the development of anxiety and phobias, there are many different approaches to treatment. However, doctors do not usually distinguish between phobias and anxiety when they treat a patient. Both conditions result from the same problem: fear. The goal of treatment is to deal with a patient's fear by finding out what is causing it and then trying to eliminate it.

There is no single answer to the question of how to deal with fear-related problems. The symptoms and severity of the conditions vary so widely from person to person that therapists, psychiatrists, and other doctors usually prefer to use a variety of methods for treatment. A technique that works for one patient may not work for another and vice versa, so no single method has been proven better than the others.

LOGICAL APPROACHES

A *logical* approach to treatment is one that attempts to help the patient eliminate fear by understanding its source. Therapists hope that when the sufferer realizes that the dread is groundless, it will eventually disappear. This does not happen immediately because, as in most types of treatment, recovery is a gradual process.

One of the most common treatments for anxiety is therapy, a method used by trained specialists to help the patient face up to and overcome his or her fears by discussing them.

The Psychoanalytic Method

One logical approach is the *psychoanalytic* method, a technique based on Freud's idea that a person's anxiety is an expression of repressed feelings about past relationships. The treatment tries to help the patient face these feelings head-on. Through talking about the patient's past, the therapist learns about situations and events that could have produced the repressed feelings. Once the patient understands where his or her fears originated, these feelings should be easier to control.

Although some therapists still use the psychoanalytic approach, other therapists question whether it is based on sound reasoning. Some modern researchers have criticized Freud's idea that Little Hans's fear of horses was based on repressed hatred of his father. In 1960, psychologists Joseph Wolpe and Stanley Rachman pointed out that most of the evidence surrounding the case was circumstantial: There was no real proof that Hans saw his father as a competitor for his mother's attentions, nor was there any solid proof that the horse represented the father. Instead, they suggest, the boy could have been terrified of the horse for some other reason. Researchers still debate Freud's conclusion in this case as well as his other theories about mental disorders.

The Cognitive Method |

Another logical approach to treating anxiety fears is the *cognitive* method. This treatment attempts to have the patient think logically about the thing he or she dreads and hence recognize that there is actually nothing to fear. For example, a phobic person is usually convinced that certain terrible things will happen as a result of contact with the dreaded object. In cognitive therapy, the patient is urged to consider whether these things will actually occur.

A cognitive therapist tells the patient to recall his or her phobic feelings and then asks such questions as "Would you disintegrate and die? Would the world stop turning? Would all your friends and relatives desert you?" In time, the patient learns to reassure him- or herself that phobic feelings will not cause these things to happen.

Filling in the Blank

In his book *Cognitive Therapy and the Emotional Disorders*, Aaron Beck explains another aspect of cognitive treatment. According to Beck, there is normally a sequence of events in a fear reaction, represented by the letters *A*, *B*, and *C*. *A* is the *stimulus*, the thing that the subject dreads. *C* is the subject's excessive response, the bout of anxiety or panic attack. Cognitive therapy concludes that sufferers often do not logically consider *B*, the hidden thought process occurring between the stimulus and the response. Beck suggests that *B* can be filled in with the logical consideration of how real the threat is.

Cognitive therapy tries to help fill in that blank, to make the patient consider just how unreasonable his or her fear is. Beck describes a person with an extreme dread of dogs, who

> became frightened when near a dog even when there was no possibility of his being attacked. He would feel nervous when a dog was chained or fenced in, or when a dog was obviously too small to injure him. I recommended that he focus on whatever thoughts occurred to him the next time he saw a dog—any dog.

This chart illustrates the success of therapy among female agoraphobes. Based on a 1987 study of recovery rates made two years after therapy was completed, it suggests that wives whose husbands accompany them into treatment show longer-lasting improvement.

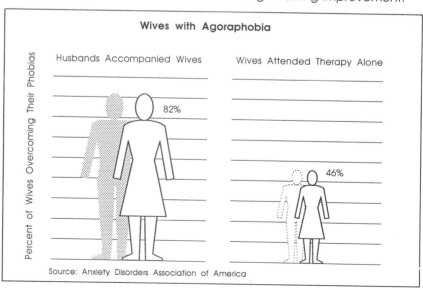

Wives with Agoraphobia

Husbands Accompanied Wives   Wives Attended Therapy Alone

Percent of Wives Overcoming Their Phobias

82%

46%

Source: Anxiety Disorders Association of America

At the next interview, the man told Beck how he had filled in the blank: Each time he encountered a dog, he thought about why he was afraid and was thus able to understand the cause of this fear. Simply put, the patient automatically believed every dog to be dangerous.

> He stated, "I realized how ridiculous it was to think that a small poodle could hurt me." He also recognized that when he saw a large dog on a leash he would think ... "The dog will jump up and bite out one of my eyes. It will jump up and bite my neck and kill me." Within three weeks, the patient was able to overcome his long-standing fear by repeatedly recognizing his thoughts when exposed to dogs.

Implosive Therapy

Another logical approach asks the patient to allow a feared event to play out in his or her mind. In *Abnormal Psychology and Modern Life*, Coleman describes different cases that used this method successfully. Therapist A. S. Frankel employed this approach to help a woman who had a disabling fear of earthquakes. The sequence of events in her terrifying scenario was always the same: She imagined that the ground was shaking, that the house was swaying back and forth, and that she was picking up her baby and trying to escape. At that point, the fear became overpowering and she was unsure of what might happen next, except that she and the baby would surely die.

In a series of therapy sessions, Frankel encouraged the woman to relive her earthquake fantasy instead of shying away from it. The therapist asked questions like "What happened next?" In time, the final outcome of her earthquake story came to light. It usually involved her climbing from the rubble, both she and her baby completely unhurt. Eventually, the woman thought less and less about earthquakes, having learned to overcome her fear. Since the technique helps a patient to envision and "explode" the fears inwardly, it is often referred to as *implosive therapy*. It is also called *imagery therapy*.

ACTIVE APPROACHES

A more active approach to treatment puts less stress on thinking and more on doing. Such techniques are based on the idea that anxiety and phobias are best dealt with by physically facing them, although not necessarily all at once. (Many experts believe that this would be too traumatic for most people and only serve to make patients more fearful.) Instead, treatment is usually gradual, a step-by-step process that allows each patient to proceed through therapy comfortably at his or her own pace.

The Gradual Approach

In 1928, professors Harold Jones and Mary Cover Jones demonstrated the gradual approach to therapy with a patient named Peter, a little boy who had a strong fear of white rabbits. The therapists began the experiment by putting a rabbit on the side of the room opposite from Peter, who sat contentedly eating some cookies. He watched the animal with some concern but decided that it was too far away to constitute a threat. In each session, the Joneses moved the rabbit a little closer to the boy. Slowly, Peter became conditioned to the presence of the creature. Eventually, it sat in his lap while he ate his cookies.

Experts call the sequence of graduated steps used in such therapy a *hierarchy*. In each case, the therapist constructs a hierarchy to suit the particular patient. As treatment progresses, if the patient reacts with a great deal of anxiety to a certain step in the hierarchy, the therapist concludes that the steps are too large. The sequence is then redesigned so the patient faces smaller, more tolerable stages of exposure to the fear.

In *Adjustment and Growth*, Spencer Rathus and Jeffrey Nevid cite an example of gradual treatment for a specific fear: A young woman had a dread of driving, making her "extremely dependent on family and friends for commuting back and forth to work, shopping, and recreational activities." The goal was to help her gain the ability to drive the 30 miles to and from work. The hierarchy of steps follows.

1. Sitting behind the wheel of her car with an understanding friend who would keep her company.

2. Sitting alone behind the wheel of her car.

3. Driving around the block with her friend in the car.

4. Driving around the block alone in the car.

5. Driving a few miles back and forth with her friend in the car.

6. Driving a few miles back and forth alone.

7. Driving the route to work and back with her friend on a non-working day.

8. Driving the route to work and back alone on a nonworking day.

9. Driving the route with her friend on a working day.

10. Driving the route alone on a working day.

When the 10th step was completed successfully, the goal was attained. The woman could drive to work alone without undue anxiety. The next goal might have been to enable her to drive alone to some more distant destination. It is important to stress that this is a general example and that the specific hierarchy presented might not necessarily

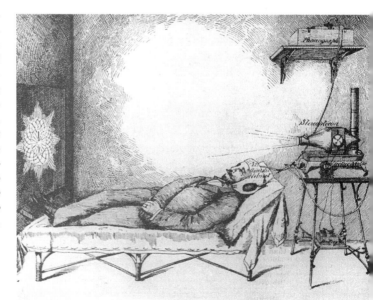

This illustration documents an early treatment for depression that used slides and music to soothe the patient. This idea is echoed today in systematic desensitization, a treatment that asks the phobic patient to relax while gradually exposing him or her to reproductions of the object he or she dreads.

work for everyone. There might be 20—or even 50—separate steps required for someone who needs an even more gradual approach. The essential factor is that the patient feel reasonably free from anxiety during the performance of each step.

Using Relaxation

A more complicated and often successful variation of the gradual behavioral method is to have the patient completely relax during each step in the hierarchy. This idea was first suggested by psychiatrist Joseph Wolpe, who called the method *systematic desensitization.*

Using this approach, a patient might lie on a couch watching a screen on which slides or films are presented by the therapist. The patient concentrates on keeping every muscle in a state of total relaxation. The images on the screen portray aspects of the thing or situation the patient fears.

For instance, if the person is terrified of snakes, various images of snakes are shown. At first, these images are mild—perhaps a snake resting on a rock 50 feet away, too far away to be a threat. When the patient can remain totally relaxed after seeing that image, the next image appears, one that shows a snake in a slightly more menacing pose. Patient and therapist then try to regain and maintain the state of relaxation again. Step by step the patient works up to being able to tolerate close-ups of snakes with fangs bared. The next phase in the treatment might then involve having the patient see and eventually even touch live snakes, all the while feeling relaxed and free from anxiety.

Systematic desensitization has become very popular with experts working to eliminate anxiety. Some, like psychologist Gordon Paul of the University of Illinois, estimate that 90% of the phobic people who have been treated using the technique have overcome their fears.

Participant Modeling

A variation of the method that has proved successful in some cases is *participant modeling.* In this approach, the patient watches someone else deal with a frightening situation in a step-by-step manner. Later, the patient imitates that model's behavior.

One example is that of therapists Paul Bourque and Robert Ladouceur, who used participant modeling to help a group of acrophobes. The subjects, whose average age was 29, avoided all high places, including balconies, bridges, fire escapes, ladders, and observation towers. The therapists modeled the desired behaviors for the patients. They began by climbing the steps of the first landing of a fire escape with six landings. Then they walked around on the landing. Next, they ventured near the edge and, eventually, looked over the edge. A final step was to look over without holding on to the railing.

The patients imitated the therapists' actions little by little, sometimes with a therapist standing alongside for reinforcement. The hierarchy of steps was repeated for each succeeding level until the patients could look down from the sixth landing with relative ease.

Flooding

A more recent type of treatment, however, takes a different approach. In the method known as *flooding*, the patient is completely immersed in the situation he or she fears most. For example, if a person is afraid of heights, the therapist would take him or her to the top of the highest building in town and have the patient lean over the edge.

Flooding therapy operates on the principle that the fear reaction can last for only a certain amount of time and then must wear off. The reaction itself cannot kill the person, unless he or she has heart trouble. Ideally, a patient can overcome the fear quite rapidly in this way. However, if an individual begins flooding treatment and becomes too frightened to follow through with it, the experience may only strengthen his or her fears. For this reason, most therapists are unwilling to try this technique.

None of the treatments described is certain to work for everyone, and often therapists may combine two or more methods. In recent years, psychiatrists have begun to recommend using drugs in conjunction with therapy. The medications that they commonly prescribe are

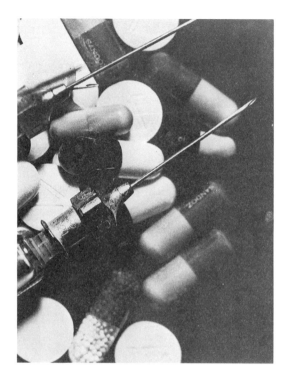

No drug is known to cure anxiety and phobic disorders, but certain medications do ease the symptoms of anxiety or panic attacks while the patient undergoes therapy. Such drugs must be taken with caution because they all can produce side effects.

not clear-cut cures for anxiety disorders. Rather, they help a troubled individual begin to gain control while therapy then reinforces this achievement.

⚕ DRUGS FOR TREATMENT

Although no drug is known to solve all of a person's difficulties with anxiety, panic attacks, or phobias, doctors hope that medications that ease the physical impact of intense fear may also prevent attacks from taking hold and causing the patient's condition to worsen.

The effectiveness of a drug depends on many factors, such as the severity of the subject's problem and the success of nondrug treatments being administered at the same time. All drugs used to treat anxiety disorders have side effects and should be taken under the continuing supervision of a physician, combined with simultaneous treatment by a therapist. None of these drugs is recommended for pregnant patients.

Tranquilizers

Tranquilizers, which have a calming effect on the body, were perhaps the first drugs used to treat anxiety. They do not, however, prevent the attacks themselves, and, unfortunately, they also have side effects. *Minor tranquilizers* include drugs with brand names such as Valium, Librium, Xanax, and Ativan. They relieve anxiety but offer only very short-term relief, which is not enough to resolve a problem that is often considered a long-term illness.

Minor tranquilizers are also physically and mentally addictive. In the case of physical addiction, a patient may experience physically painful withdrawal symptoms when he or she stops using the drug. In the case of mental addiction, the patient may believe that he or she needs the drug in order to feel comfortable and safe from future problems.

Major tranquilizers, such as Thorazine and Haldol, are typically used to treat patients suffering from a *psychosis*, a mental illness that causes the victim to lose touch with reality. However, these drugs were

These ads are used to introduce the brand name of a pharmaceutical company that manufactures both tranquilizers and antidepressants. Tranquilizers are able to produce a calming effect on the body, whereas antidepressants relieve the symptoms of panic attacks.

not intended for use in treating anxiety disorders, and many experts believe they do not help them. Some doctors even feel that major tranquilizers actually increase anxiety—especially because the side effects include agitation, dry mouth, and tremors.

Antidepressants

In recent years, another group of drugs, called *antidepressants* because they were first developed to treat depression, has been found to ease anxiety. These medications offer more relief than do tranquilizers because they suppress panic attacks. Unfortunately, their side effects are also more severe, often bringing on insomnia, shakiness, and irritability.

Antidepressants are further divided into two groups. One of these, the *tricyclics*, includes Elavil and Tofranil. Tricyclic antidepressant drugs are generally used to treat severe depression. Perhaps the best-known member of this group is *imipramine*. In general, tricyclics cause such side effects as dry mouth, constipation, and dizziness. These drugs can also irritate the heart to the point of triggering seizures. A new drug in this group, *trazodone*, may cause drowsiness at first, but is found to work when similar drugs fail. However, it is still being tested.

The other group of antidepressant drugs is the *MAO inhibitors* (monoamine oxidase inhibitors). Experts tend to agree that the single most effective MAO inhibitor is *phenelzine*, commonly marketed as Nardil. These medications are difficult to prescribe and to regulate, posing an especially dangerous problem because they tend to increase blood pressure. Another disadvantage is that the patient should not eat foods containing *tyramine*, a substance often found in cheese, beer, and nuts, because it tends to increase blood pressure.

It can take three to four weeks for an antidepressant drug to start having a positive effect on the patient. After recovery begins, the patient is usually kept on the medication another 6 to 12 months while therapy continues. Throughout the treatment, the doctor must continually monitor the patient's progress and adjust the dosage accordingly. The choice of which drug to use depends on finding the greatest improvement with the fewest side effects.

Other Medications

One of the newer drugs, *alprazolam*, is often one of the first that doctors will use to help a patient suffering from anxiety. Although it is categorized technically with the *benzodiazepine* drugs, the group that includes minor tranquilizers, this medication is more useful because it also prevents panic attacks from occurring. Moreover, it works quickly—within a few days—and has relatively few side effects. Nevertheless, it does cause drowsiness and must be taken more frequently than its counterparts.

This chart illustrates the lack of treatment for those who suffer from anxiety disorders. Although the problem is one of the most common and treatable mental disorders, only one out of every four sufferers receives adequate attention.

Source: Anxiety Disorders Association of America

Beta Blockers

Other substances, *beta blockers*, are usually administered to heart patients who suffer from high blood pressure and irregular heartbeat. The most commonly known beta blocker is *propranolol.* Although these drugs do not treat phobias specifically, they can work to alleviate the symptoms.

Beta blockers offer relief to agoraphobes, who dread the symptoms of panic attacks more than anything else, by decreasing the patient's heart rate, blood pressure, and trembling hands. This medication also helps those agoraphobes who have specific fears of an increased heart rate, although this typically alleviates only one of many fears. Yet once the drug is withdrawn, agoraphobes have made no real progress at overcoming the fear.

The use of beta blockers to relieve phobias has not been studied in great depth. However, one study which specifically looked at their effect on severe stage fright has shown they are helpful in reducing such problems as trembling fingers, sweaty palms, and memory loss.

THE IMPORTANCE OF TREATMENT

Although great strides have been made to provide drug and other therapies, specialists are still working to unlock the mystery to the brain's inner workings. Treatments for anxiety and phobias can be complex, and this overview presents a brief look at the many types of help that are available for these conditions. Unfortunately, many sufferers either do not know that treatments exist or are embarrassed to seek help. Yet symptoms of anxiety or phobias strike millions of people and should not be considered a cause for shame.

Anyone who suffers from unreasonable fears should not hesitate to seek professional help. Often a family doctor can recommend a good local therapist, or a nearby hospital will offer a list of specialists who practice in the vicinity. The most difficult part of recovery may be taking that first step and asking for help, yet therein lies the key to a freer and happier life.

APPENDIX I:
FOR MORE INFORMATION

The following is a list of organizations that can provide further information about anxiety disorders and phobias.

GENERAL INFORMATION

American Psychiatric Association
1400 K Street NW
Washington, DC 20005
(202) 682-6000

American Psychological Association
1200 17th Street NW
Washington, DC 20036
(202) 955-7600

Anxiety Disorders Center
c/o Carol Lindemann, Ph.D.
245 East 87th Street
New York, NY 10128
(212) 860-5560

Freedom from Fear Foundation
P.O. Box 1500-1302
Toronto, Ontario M9C 4V5
Canada
(416) 761-6006

Phobia and Anxiety Disorders Clinic
State University of New York at Albany
1535 Western Avenue
Albany, NY 12203
(518) 456-4127

AGORAPHOBIA

Agoraphobic Treatment Program
Sheppard Pratt Hospital
6501 North Charles Street
Towson, MD 21285
(301) 823-8200

C.A.L.L. (Concerned Agoraphobics
Learning to Live)
380 Tolosa Way
San Luis Obispo, CA 93405
(805) 543-3764

TERRAP National Headquarters
(Territorial Apprehensiveness)
648 Menlo Avenue, #5
Menlo Park, CA 94025
(415) 327-1312

FEAR OF FLYING

Fly Without Fear
310 Madison Avenue
New York, NY 10017
(212) 697-7666

APPENDIX II:
PHOBIAS AND THEIR
SCIENTIFIC NAMES

FEAR OF	PHOBIA
being buried alive	taphephobia
bridges	gephyrophobia
children, dolls	pediophobia
color	chromatophobia
crossing streets	dromophobia
death	thanatophobia
dust	amathophobia
eating	phagophobia
everything	panphobia
failure	kakorrhaphiophobia
fog	homichlophobia
frogs	batrachophobia
ghosts	phasmophobia
glass	crystallophobia
God	theophobia
hell	hadephobia
lightning	astraphobia
men	androphobia
mice	musophobia
money	chrematophobia
the number 13	triskaidekaphobia
rain	ombrophobia
robbers	harpaxophobia
school	school phobia
sleep	hypnophobia
snow	chionphobia
string	linonophobia
sunlight	heliophobia
trains	siderodromophobia
vaccination	vaccinophobia
walking	basiphobia
women	gynophobia

FURTHER READING

GENERAL INFORMATION

Agras, Stewart. *Panic: Facing Fears, Phobias, and Anxiety.* New York: Freeman, 1985.

Aronson, Marvin L. *How to Overcome Your Fear of Flying.* New York: Hawthorn Books, 1971.

Barlow, David H. *Anxiety and Its Disorders: The Nature and Treatment of Anxiety Panic.* New York: Guilford Press, 1988.

Beck, Aaron T. *Cognitive Therapy and the Emotional Disorders.* New York: International Universities Press, 1976.

Beck, Aaron T., and Gary Emery. *Anxiety Disorders and Phobias: A Cognitive Perspective.* New York: Basic Books, 1985.

Bourne, Ed. *The Anxiety and Phobia Workbook.* Oakland: New Harbinger, 1990.

Cameron, Norman, and Joseph F. Rychlak. *Personality Development and Psychopathology: A Dynamic Approach.* Boston: Houghton Mifflin, 1985.

Clarke, J. Christopher, and Arthur Jackson. *Hypnosis and Behavior Therapy: The Treatment of Anxiety Panic.* New York: Springer Publishing, 1983.

Coleman, James C., et al. *Abnormal Psychology and Modern Life.* Glenview, IL: Scott, Foresman, 1980.

Drews, Toby R. *Getting Rid of Anxiety and Stress.* South Plainsfield, NJ: Bridge Publications, 1982.

Dupont, Robert L., ed. *Phobia: A Comprehensive Summary of Modern Treatments.* New York: Brunner-Mazel, 1982.

Filson, Brent. *There's a Monster in Your Closet! Understanding Phobias.* Englewood Cliffs, NJ: Messner, 1986.

Fried, Barbara. *Who's Afraid? The Phobic's Handbook.* Rev. ed. New York: Gardner Press, 1985.

Gittleman, Rachel, ed. *Anxiety Disorders of Childhood.* New York: Guilford Press, 1986.

Goldstein, Alan, and Berry Stainback. *Overcoming Agoraphobia.* New York: Viking Press, 1987.

Goldstein, Michael J., and James O. Palmer. *The Experience of Anxiety: A Casebook.* New York: Oxford University Press, 1975.

Goodwin, Donald W. *Phobia: The Facts.* New York: Oxford University Press, 1983.

Griest, John H., et al. *Anxiety and Its Treatment.* New York: Warner Books, 1987.

Henley, Arthur. *Phobias: The Crippling Fears.* New York: Carol, 1987.

Hunt, Douglas. *No More Fears.* New York: Warner Books, 1988.

Marks, Isaac. *Fears, Phobias, and Rituals: Panic, Anxiety, and Their Disorders.* New York: Oxford University Press, 1987.

———. *Cure and Care of Neuroses: Theory and Practice of Behavioural Psychotherapy.* New York: John Wiley & Sons, 1981.

Millman, Howard L., et al. *Therapies for Adults: Depressive, Anxiety, and Personality Disorders.* San Francisco: Jossey-Bass, 1982.

Olshan, Neal, and Julie Wang. *Everything You Wanted to Know About Phobias but Were Afraid to Ask.* New York: Beaufort Books, 1981.

Rachman, S. *Phobias: Their Nature and Control.* Springfield, IL: Thomas, 1968.

Rathus, Spencer A., and Jeffrey S. Nevid. *Adjustment and Growth: The Challenges of Life.* New York: Holt, Rinehart & Winston, 1980.

Sagan, Carl. *The Dragons of Eden.* New York: Ballantine Books, 1977.

Sheehan, David V. *The Anxiety Disease.* New York: Bantam Books, 1986.

Stein, Sara. *About Phobias.* New York: Walker, 1984.

Weekes, Claire. *Hope and Help for Your Nerves.* New York: Bantam Books, 1978.

—————. *Peace from Nervous Suffering.* New York: Bantam Books, 1983.

Whitehead, Tony. *Fears and Phobias.* New York: Arco, 1983.

Wolpe, Joseph M., and David Wolpe. *Life Without Fear: Anxiety and Its Cure.* Oakland: New Harbinger, 1988.

Zane, Manuel D., and Harry Milt. *Your Phobia: Understanding Your Fears Through Contextual Therapy.* Washington, DC: American Psychiatric Press, 1984.

GLOSSARY

agoraphobia *agora*, marketplace + *phobos*, fear; an unpredictable, extreme dread that strikes the sufferer and does not subside until he or she has reached the safety of home; agoraphobes usually suffer from two or more phobias and therefore feel threatened from many directions until they can retreat to their isolated refuge

alprazolam a member of the benzodiazepine group of drugs; used to prevent panic attacks

anticipatory anxiety an extreme dread of the possibility of suffering a panic attack

antidepressants drugs used to relieve or prevent severe depression and to ease some cases of anxiety

anxiety a sense of apprehension and fear due to the anticipation of an impending negative situation; sometimes marked by sweating, tension, and increased pulse

anxiety attack a condition of extreme anxiety when one feels a loss of control; also called a panic attack

beta blockers substances that regulate heartbeat in cardiac patients; also sometimes used to alleviate the symptoms of panic attacks

benzodiazepine a depressant that is a potent reliever of anxiety and insomnia

catecholamine a natural stimulant released by the nerve endings; excess amounts of the chemical are found in individuals who are overly anxious

cognitive method a method used to treat anxiety in which the patient is taught to think logically about what he or she dreads and to recognize that there is really nothing to fear

conditioning learning by watching a repeated behavior

depressant an agent that lowers the activity or strength of a bodily function

depression a condition marked by sadness, inactivity, an increased difficulty in thinking and concentrating, and feelings of hopelessness and dejection

displacement redirecting an emotion or fear from one object to another; according to Freud's theory, all phobias are the consequence of displaced anxiety resulting from poor parent-child relationships

flooding a type of phobia treatment in which the sufferer is exposed to and completely immersed in the situation he or she fears

generalized anxiety disorder excessive anxiety due to worry over a possible but unlikely misfortune; symptoms may include increased heart rate, shortness of breath, dizziness, irritability, and insomnia

gradual approach a method of phobia treatment in which the patient follows a sequence of graduated steps that expose him to the object he fears and enable him to overcome the phobia

hierarchy the sequence of steps used in the gradual approach to phobia therapy; each step exposes the patient to a slightly more threatening degree of the feared object in order to slowly bring the individual closer to overcoming his or her fear

hypochondria an abnormal concern for one's health that frequently involves imaginary illnesses

implosive therapy imagery therapy; a type of treatment that helps the sufferer overcome a particular fear by carrying out the feared encounter in his or her mind

inhibitory neurotransmitters natural tranquilizers released by the body to relieve anxiety

instinct an inborn tendency for an organism to react in certain ways without thought to specific stimuli

lactic acid a substance formed in the muscles during exercise; people suffering from anxiety have shown an unusually high concentration of lactic acid in their blood

MAO inhibitors monoamine oxidase inhibitors; one of two types of antidepressants used to ease anxiety; side effects include raised blood pressure and an increased sensitivity to foods containing tyramine, a substance found in cheese, beer, and nuts

modeling the theory that children can develop their fears and phobias by watching adults with similar problems

nerve ending the part of the nerve that releases chemical messengers called neurotransmitters in order to transmit impulses through the body

neurosis a mental and emotional disorder with no discernible cause; different from a psychosis, in which the victim loses touch with reality

neurotransmitter a chemical that carries nerve signals across gaps between nerve cells

obsessive phobia persistent thoughts causing extreme irrational fear; often includes a fear of becoming contaminated or of losing control and performing some violent act

panic attack an extreme reaction to fear in which a person loses self-control, acts irrationally, and often believes that death is near; also called an anxiety attack

participant modeling an approach to anxiety therapy in which the patient watches the therapist deal with a frightening situation and then tries to imitate the therapist's behavior

phobia a persistent, irrational, disabling fear of an object, activity, or situation

psychiatrist a physician who diagnoses and treats mental disorders and can prescribe drugs as part of therapy

psychoanalytic method a technique used to relieve anxiety and phobias in which a therapist determines, by evaluating an individual's repressed feelings, what might have triggered his or her fears

psychologist an individual who treats both normal and abnormal mental processes and studies the science of the mind and behavior

psychosis a mental disorder that causes an individual to lose touch with reality and often includes hallucinations and delusions

repression holding back or burying feelings, often negative ones, for a long period of time; can eventually lead to a state of severe anxiety

social phobia a phobia that involves people or public situations

specific phobia extreme fear of a single, known situation, activity, or object; also called simple phobia

stimulus a change in the environment that evokes a response in an organism

subconscious the part of the mental processes that takes place below the surface of consciousness, without the individual's awareness that it occurs

sympathetic nervous system the part of the nervous system that governs the body's automatic responses to pain, anger, and fear

systematic desensitization a variation of the gradual approach to phobia therapy that focuses on maintaining a state of total relaxation at each step of the hierarchy

tranquilizers drugs that have a soothing effect on the body; minor tranquilizers offer short-term relief from anxiety; major tranquilizers are used to treat patients suffering from a psychosis but also produce various side effects, including agitation, dry mouth, and tremors

tricyclics one of two types of antidepressants used to ease anxiety; may have side effects such as dry mouth, constipation, dizziness, and seizures

INDEX

PICTURE CREDITS

Don Nardo is a writer, actor, filmmaker, and composer. He has written articles, short stories, and more than 20 books, as well as screenplays and teleplays, including work for Warner Bros. and ABC television. He has appeared in dozens of stage productions and has worked in front of or behind the camera in 20 films. His musical compositions, such as his oratorio *Richard III* and his film score for a version of *The Time Machine,* have been played by regional orchestras. Mr. Nardo lives with his wife on Cape Cod, Massachusetts.

Solomon H. Snyder, M.D., is Distinguished Service Professor of Neuroscience, Pharmacology, and Psychiatry and director of the Department of Neuroscience at the Johns Hopkins University School of Medicine. He has served as president of the Society for Neuroscience and in 1978 received the Albert Lasker Award in Medical Research for his discovery of opiate receptors in the brain. Dr. Snyder is a member of the National Academy of Sciences and a Fellow of the American Academy of Arts and Sciences. He is the author of *Drugs and the Brain, Uses of Marijuana, Madness and the Brain, The Troubled Mind*, and *Biological Aspects of Mental Disorder*. He is also the general editor of Chelsea House's ENCYCLOPEDIA OF PSYCHOACTIVE DRUGS.

C. Everett Koop, M.D., Sc.D., is former Surgeon General, deputy assistant secretary for health, and director of the Office of International Health of the U.S. Public Health Service. A pediatric surgeon with an international reputation, he was previously surgeon-in-chief of Children's Hospital of Philadelphia and professor of pediatric surgery and pediatrics at the University of Pennsylvania. Dr. Koop is the author of more than 175 articles and books on the practice of medicine. He has served as surgery editor of the *Journal of Clinical Pediatrics* and editor-in-chief of the *Journal of Pediatric Surgery*. Dr. Koop has received nine honorary degrees and numerous other awards, including the Denis Brown Gold Medal of the British Association of Paediatric Surgeons, the William E. Ladd Gold Medal of the American Academy of Pediatrics, and the Copernicus Medal of the Surgical Society of Poland. He is a chevalier of the French Legion of Honor and a member of the Royal College of Surgeons, London.